Sprouting
for all
seasons

How and What to Sprout,
Including Delicious, Easy-to-Prepare Recipes

Bertha B. Larimore

Horizon Publishers

Fifth Printing, May 1993

International Standard Book Number
0-88290-055-2

Library of Congress Card Catalog Number
75-23564

Horizon Publishers' Catalog and Order Number
1203

Printed and distributed
in the United States of America by

Horizon
Publishers
& Distributors, Incorporated
P.O. Box 490 Bountiful, Utah 84011-0490

DEDICATED TO

MY MOTHER, EMMA ROGERS BURNHAM,

WHO TAUGHT ME

THE JOY OF FINE COOKING

PHOTOGRAPHS

BY

KENNETH C. BEAUDRIE

ABOUT THE AUTHOR

Bertha Burnham Larimore has had a lifelong interest in cooking which began with her collecting recipes when she was a teenager. Her mother was an outstanding cook and taught her many of the fine points about cooking. She has used her creative abilities to develop many unusual and delicious recipes, and is well-known for her expert cooking and prize-winning recipes. Mrs. Larimore was a Utah State finalist in the 1961 Pillsbury Bake-Off, and also placed third on a Western Family Recipe contest. She has won numerous local and state recipe and cooking contests both in Utah and California.

It was while living in California that she became interested in nutrition and sprouting. For two years she attended nutrition classes in the Los Angeles area taught by nutritionist Adelle Davis. Her experience with sprouting spans more than 20 years. Her firsthand knowledge of sprouting was gained by growing, preparing and serving sprouts in delicious, nutritious meals to her husband and three children. Her interest in sprouting and cooking led her to convert and develop many of her prize-winning recipes to include the use of sprouts. With this background, *"Sprouting For All Seasons,"* was inevitable.

Mrs. Larimore is also the author of the humorous book, *Kids Tell It Like It Is!* Other literary attainments include short stories, researched articles, serious poetry and light verse. Her writings have been published in Parent's Magazine, Better Camping, Humorama, In Magazine and the Family Weekly. She has supplied material for movie and television personality Phyllis Diller, and her light verse and serious poetry were published in the 1974 Golden Anniversary Edition of "Utah Sings," An Anthology of Contemporary Verse. She has won many writing awards in national and state writing contests. *Sprouting For All Seasons* is her second published book.

Mrs. Larimore is also a talented artist and has won ribbons and awards for her oil paintings of landscapes, seascapes, mountains and deserts. She uses her ability as a public speaker to present a humorous and entertaining review of her book, *"Kids Tell It Like It Is!"* before literary and private clubs, libraries, church, civic and school groups.

The author resides in Roy, Utah and is presently employed as a Military Education Counselor in the Hill Air Force Base Education Office. Her other hobbies include knitting, sewing, gardening and traveling.

TABLE OF CONTENTS

4

Soy Sprout Creole; Sauteed Lentil Sprouts;
Sprout Succotash.

Chewy Soy Oatmeal Cookies; Soy Crunchies;
Currant Icebox Beanies; Peanut Butter Bean Balls;
Orange Bean Sprout Drops; Molasses Sprout
Cookies; Soy Almond Cookies; Dutch Apple
Sprout Pie; Pinto Sprout Harvest Pie; Soy Sprout
Pie; Apple Crunch; Cranberry Soy Sprout Crunch;
Golden Honey Custard; Fresh Apple-Soy Cake;
Vanilla Sauce; Pinto Pineapple Cake; Caramel
Frosting.

Soy Nut Fruit Balls; Soy Peanut Butter Chews;
Soy Nut Brittle; Cracker Jack Popcorn; Garlic-
Buttered Popcorn and Soy Nuts; Soy Butterscotch Clusters; Soy Carob Fudge; Sprout Fondant.

INTRODUCTION

Although relatively few people sprout seeds, and many have never heard of the practice, sprouting is many centuries old. Sprouts were first mentioned in a book by the Emperor of China in 2939 B.C. They probably had been used by the Chinese long before that time. Mung beans are the oldest and best known of all sprouts, and have been used by the Chinese for nearly 5,000 years. Today they are still a very important part of Chinese cuisine.

Sprouting is not a mysterious, complicated procedure, but a simple task requiring very little time or expense. A glass jar, a piece of nylon net or cheese cloth, a rubber band, and a few seeds are all that it takes to start a "sprout garden." With this simple equipment, a beginner can produce enough sprouts right in the kitchen to supply the needs of a family. The actual time required would probably amount to no more than 10 minutes each day for this profitable and rewarding experience.

Sprouting is becoming more popular every day, and those who become involved regret that they didn't begin years earlier. There are many good reasons for sprouting seeds—they taste delicious, are highly nutritious and improve health, save time and money, are low in calories, give quick energy and are an important addition to the home food storage programs.

There are dozens of different seeds, grains and legumes that can be successfully sprouted, and several different methods of sprouting. The individual seeds and methods of sprouting are discussed in detail in this book, and an effort has been made to simplify procedures, so that even a beginner will have success.

CHAPTER I

REASONS FOR SPROUTING

Sprouts Have Good Taste and Variety

There are many good reasons for sprouting seeds and grains, but the fact that they are absolutely delicious to the taste is reason enough to add them to the diet. Anyone who enjoys raw vegetables and salads will enjoy sprouts. They are also a delightful and unusual addition to cooked dishes, breads, casseroles and soups. There is nothing more delicious or nutritious than a loaf of sprouted wheat or rye bread. Many sprouts have a very high protein content and can be used as meat extenders or substitutes. There are dozens of different seeds and grains that can be sprouted, and each one has a different taste and texture. Beginners should try as many varieties and combinations as possible to find which are the most pleasing to the individual taste.

Some raw sprouts, including Alaskan peas and soybean, have a taste similar to fresh garden peas. They may be steamed a few minutes and served with butter as a cooked vegetable. Lentils have a crisp, nutty texture with a flavor resembling fresh ground pepper. They are at their best when added to fresh, green salads.

For maximum nutritional benefit, sprouts are best eaten raw. However, they retain most of their nutritional qualities even when cooked. They may be steamed, roasted, fried, pureed, ground, or served in cream sauces and gravies, making them suitable for small children and those on bland diets.

Sprouts also retain most of their nutritional value when dried in a warm oven. Grind them in the blender for a few seconds after they are dry and store the powder in air-tight jars. They keep well in a cool place and can be used in baking, beverages, desserts, and spreads. They are especially valuable when stirred into baby food.

With such an endless variety of sprouts and recipes from which to choose, delicious meals and snacks can be prepared to please everyone.

Sprouts Improve Health

In the sprouting process there is a dramatic increase in the vitamin and mineral content of seeds, beans and grains, For instance, the dry soybean has no Vitamin C. After sprouting for 72 hours, Dr. Pauline Berry Mack, at the University of Pennsylvania, found that one-half cup of the sprouts contained as much Vitamin C as six glasses of orange juice. Dr. Paul Burkholder, Yale University, sprouted oats for five days and discovered that the B Vitamins had skyrocketed—500% more B6, 600% more folic acid, 10% more B1 and 135% more B2 than before sprouting. Sprouted oats also have 600% more Vitamin C than unsprouted ones. Further studies with sprouted seeds show similar spectacular results, and confirm that they are an excellent source of the important vitamins and minerals— all in natural forms which can be readily assimilated by the body.

The protein content of seeds is usually increased during the sprouting process. The sprout proteins are converted to amino acids and can be more readily assimilated by the body. In fact, the eight essential amino acids are present in many sprouts, making them a good source of high-quality, complete protein. Some sprouts are lacking in one or more amino acids, but when two or three different kinds of sprouts are eaten at the same meal, they can combine and form a complete protein. The people of Mexico and other countries eat corn tortillas and beans at the same meal to supply a complete protein.

Sprouts are also a source of quick energy. In the sprouting process, the starches are converted to simple sugars which rapidly enter the bloodstream when sprouts are eaten. Sprouted seeds contain the enzymes which control the chemical reactions in the body. These enzymes must be replaced in the body by eating fresh garden produce. Sprouts are a dependable, inexpensive way to replenish them.

Successful studies have been conducted by doctors and scientists in India, China, England and Europe on the use of germinated seeds to prevent or cure scurvy, beri-beri, malnutrition, infertility and other nutritional deficiency diseases. Enough scientific research has been made on the sprouted seed to confirm that it is one of the most valuable and nutritious foods that can be eaten.

Sprouts are also low in calories. Most of them contain no more than 16 calories per cup. Thus a dieter could satisfy his protein, mineral and vitamin requirements with sprouts, and eliminate the usual high-calorie protein foods. With such a large variety from which to choose, diets do not become monotonous. Lentils, peas and soybeans are higher in calories than other sprouts, but since they are also high in protein, it is wise to use them also. They contain approximately 65 calories per cup, but four ounces of these sprouts yield twice as much protein as four ounces of meat. Weight for weight, soybeans yield four times as much protein as eggs.

Sprouts Save Money

Another very important reason for sprouting is to save money. Families who once get the "sprout habit" will never again go back to canned or frozen vegetables, if they have a choice.

Costs vary, depending on the amount and type of seeds purchased, but even the most expensive sprouts would probably cost no more than $.05 or $.06 per serving. For those who buy in large quantities, the cost would be reduced even more—in some cases it could be less than $.01. For instance, one pound of dry beans will yield at least eight pounds of sprouts. One pound of sprouts will serve six to eight people, which means there will be 48 to 64 servings for the cost of one pound of beans! One and one-half tablespoons of alfalfa seed will yield approximately one quart of greened sprouts, while three tablespoons of mung beans will make one quart of bean sprouts.

Lentils, peas, dry beans and soybeans are high in protein— 20 to 25%. Soybeans range from 33 to 42% protein. They can be used as meat extenders or substitutes, thus drastically cutting the high cost of meat.

If seeds are sprouted and regularly served, the food budget can be reduced without sacrificing the quality of food or the family health.

Sprouts Save Time

The time required to maintain a variety of fresh sprouts at all times is minimal. Once the equipment and seeds are on hand and the routine of soaking, rinsing and sprouting established, ten or fifteen minutes a day is all the time needed to care for a "sprout garden." It takes no weeding, fertilizing, hoeing, spraying or working long hours in the hot sun. Winter or summer, regardless of blistering sun, freezing weather, wind, rain or snow, the sprouts will continue to grow. When vacation time comes around or an out-of-town emergency arises, there is no worry about having friends or neighbors come to care for the garden.

Since sprouts are eaten fresh, there is no requirement to pick, can or preserve them. Nor is packaging, labeling, transporting and storing necessary. It takes only two to six days to produce sprouts, so if they are continually kept growing, there is no need to go to the market in order to have a supply of low-cost, fresh vegetables on hand at all times. Sprouts are worth many times the small amount of time and effort involved in growing them.

Sprouts Provide Ecological Savings

When sprouts are grown at home, the cost of planting, growing, harvesting, processing, packaging and transportation has been greatly reduced. The use of diesel fuel, concrete highways, gas, electricity and human labor has also been drastically cut.

It takes only a fraction of the amount of natural and human resources to sprout a pound of beans at home compared to purchasing that same amount in the supermarket after it has been cooked, canned, frozen or packed fresh. Not only has the middleman been eliminated with a substantial saving in the food bill, but the saving in natural and human resources is a worthwhile contribution to the ecology. Furthermore, there are practically no inedible parts, waste, cans or packages to throw into the garbage or disposal.

If seeds are sprouted and used only as needed, there will be no loss of vitamins and minerals or spoilage of food that must be thrown out, as so often happens with fresh produce in a market. Sprouts can be harvested at their peak of goodness. They are always clean and contain no preservatives, additives, poisonous sprays or insects. Sprouting at home is a dependable source for a constant supply of low-cost, high quality fresh produce.

Sprouts Aid in Emergencies and Home Storage

Every family should have a planned home storage food program. There is always the possibility of accident, illness or unemployment. Earthquakes, floods, tornadoes and other disasters may strike anywhere or anytime.

Many families already have some of the basic items to sustain life in an emergency, such as grains (wheat, rice, etc.), dry beans, powdered milk, honey, sugar, molasses and salt. In addition, canned, dried, dehydrated, and freeze-dried foods are also stored.

Fresh produce is something that cannot be stored. In an emergency when fresh produce is not available, sprouts can be the answer. Seeds take little storage space, keep well, are inexpensive and easy to obtain. Sprouts can be produced any season of the year and are ready within two to six days, and may be sprouted only as needed.

CHAPTER II

SEEDS AND GRAINS FOR SPROUTING

Buying and Storing

When buying seeds for sprouting, make certain they haven't been chemically treated in any way. Select only those sold for sprouting purposes. Seeds sold in seed and feed stores or nurseries are often for growing purposes only, and may have been chemically treated with insecticides to protect them from disease when planted in soil. If buying from these sources, be sure to ask if they have been treated, and indicate that they are to be sprouted. However, some seed stores handle seeds specifically grown for sprouting, which have not been chemically treated in any way. These are usually good sources, especially for buying larger quantities. Seeds sold in the markets are usually for food purposes and often contain cracked and broken seeds and may not sprout at all.

Local health food stores generally stock seeds for sprouting and are often a good source for small quantities. Some specialty stores may also carry them. Seeds for sprouting can be ordered by mail from reliable seed companies, but one should always specify that the seeds are for sprouting. Postage is high, however, so if possible get them from a local source.

Seeds must be stored in moisture-proof containers in a dry place. Metal, plastic or glass containers with tight-fitting lids are suitable. Date and label each container and rotate them, always using the oldest ones first. Seeds stored in a cool, dark place will keep longer than those on a warm kitchen shelf. They may also be stored in the refrigerator, if containers are absolutely moisture-proof. Seeds from the current year's crop will germinate better than the older ones. This is especially true of soybeans.

Contrary to popular belief, seeds will not store indefinitely and still germinate successfully. Many seeds have a very low percent of viability after the first year. For this reason there is a Federal Government requirement that seeds must have a germination test and be labeled, showing the year in which they are packaged. This test is good for only nine months, and if seeds are held over another year, they must be retested. Seed stores must comply with this regulation, in order that buyers are assured of quality seeds. State Departments of Agriculture, under the U. S. Department of Agriculture, have this responsibility. Always read labels and check with knowledgeable individuals at the source of purchase to be sure of fresh, viable seeds. Store no more than a year's supply.

Types to Choose

Practically all seeds, grains and legumes can be sprouted. Mung beans, alfalfa, lentils, peas, wheat and rye are some of those most often used. But don't settle for only the common ones. Since there are so many varieties with completely different tastes and textures, try as many as possible and decide on the ones most pleasing to each individual or family. Buy and store those that will be used and enjoyed.

Amounts to Buy

For the beginner, it is best to buy the small packages. Health food stores usually carry one-fourth, one-half and one-pound packages. But if sprouts are going to be a regular addition to the everyday diet, then it is much more economical to purchase seeds in larger quantities. Amounts and yield are given for each type of seed in Chapter VI, *Specific Instructions for Sprouting Individual Seeds.* A little experimenting will help determine how many and what kind of sprouts a family will use each week.

For storage programs, information concerning amounts and type of seeds to store is given in Chapter VII, *Dehydrated Foods and Sprouts—Home Storage Programs.*

Groups of Related Seeds

There are certain seeds that have similar characteristics. These are grouped on page 18. In many cases the same rules can be used for sprouting, harvesting and in recipes for all seeds in the group. However, read directions for the individual seed for special instructions and methods of sprouting. Best results are usually obtained by sprouting seeds separately, but similar-type seeds can sometimes be combined for a change of taste in sprouts. For instance, sprinkle a few garden cress seeds in with the alfalfa. Combining seeds is a good way to use up small leftover quantities.

SMALL SEEDS: Alfalfa, Clover, Millet, Sesame
GRAINS: Barley, Oats, Rye, Wheat, Triticali
TENDER BEANS: Mung Beans, Lentils
HARD BEANS: Adzuki, Black, Garden Peas, Garbanzo
   or Chick Peas, Kidney, Navy, Pinto, Red, Soybeans,
   White, and other hard beans.
GELATINOUS SEEDS: Chia Seeds, Flax, Garden Cress
VEGETABLE SEEDS: Cabbage, Cauliflower, Broccoli,
   Brussels Sprouts, Mustard, Turnips, Beets, Chard, Endive,
   Lettuce, Radish, etc.

CHAPTER III

BASIC RULES FOR SPROUTING

High-Quality Seeds

Always use high-quality seeds for sprouting. Measure, re-move chaff, broken or cracked seeds. Wash the seeds thoroughly and place them in a jar to soak in 70° to 80° water overnight in a warm, dark place. Use about four times as much water as seeds, or enough to cover them as they swell. Next morning, pour off the soak water. This water contains vitamins and minerals, and some enthusiasts save it for use in soups or beverages. Others use it for watering house plants. Rinse the sprouts and drain well. Always rinse in cold water and then in warm water for faster sprouting.

Soaking Time

Most seeds should be soaked overnight, or 8 to 12 hours. However, small seeds need be soaked no longer than two or three hours. A few seeds, including gelatinous ones, should not be soaked at all. Mung beans and some of the hard beans need a longer soaking period. Specific instructions for individual seeds are given in Chapter VI.

Moisture and Temperature

If using the jar in which the seeds were soaked for a sprout-ing container, place a piece of nylon net or cheesecloth over the mouth of the jar and secure it with jar ring or rubber band, or use plastic screen and a jar ring. If using another sprouting meth-od, place seeds in an appropriate sprouting container, following instructions given for that method. Keep the sprouts in a warm, dark place such as a cupboard or closet. The temperature should range between 68° and 80°; however, 72° is best for most sprouts. Rinse the sprouts with clear water and drain them well every four to six hours. If that is not possible, rinse the sprouts in the morning, also in the evening, and again at bedtime. Let them stand for a few minutes in cool water when they are rinsed in the evening. This allows them to soak up water if they haven't been watered during the day. In cold weather they can be rinsed again in warm water and drained well before returning them to a dark corner. Keep sprouts moist but not wet. Seeds must not stand in water or they will sour and have to be discarded.

Air Circulation

Be sure there is at least one third of the space left in the container for good circulation of air while they are growing. The amount of seed used will depend on the size of container and type of seed. Once seeds have been measured and it is determined just how many each container can hold, there will be no difficulty in overcrowding the sprouts.

Length of Time for Various Seeds

The proper length of time required for sprouts to reach desirable growth for harvesting varies with different seeds. Some seeds, and especially grains and beans, can be used within 24 hours, or as soon as the sprout appears. Others may take 72 hours or five or six days to reach maturity. If seeds are sprouted too long, they begin to grow roots—they lose their flavor and become bitter. Vitamins and minerals are also lost if sprouts are allowed to become too old. As a rule, most sprouts should be used by the time they are five or six days old. Read the instructions on individual seeds for specific sprouting times.

Important Rules To Remember

Sprouting will be successful if sprouts are kept moist; if they are kept warm; if they are kept in the dark; if they are rinsed often and have enough space for growth and good air circulation. Other important points to remember: do not let sprouts or seeds stand in water; do not let them dry out; do not sprout large amounts or fill the container too full; and above all, do not give up! It may take a little experimenting and several attempts, but learning to sprout seeds successfully is well worth the time and effort involved.

CHAPTER IV

HARVESTING AND STORING SPROUTS

Wash and Drain

Most sprouts are at their peak and contain maximum amounts of vitamins and minerals if eaten within 60 to 72 hours after germinating. However, some of the grain sprouts are best if used when the shoot is no longer than the seed itself. This is particularly important if they are to be used in breads or baked products. This may take as little as 24 hours sprouting time. Mung beans, garbanzo and soybeans can be used from the time they are ¼ inch in length. Alfalfa is best from 1 to 2 inches and greened in indirect light. Refer to individual seed for specific harvesting instructions.

Before storing, empty sprouts into a pan or sink full of cold water. Handle gently so delicate shoots will not be damaged or broken. At this time the hulls of the seeds will usually float to the top and can be removed. Also discard any hard seeds that did not sprout or any soft or brown sprouts. Lift sprouts into large strainer or colander and drain for an hour or two. Or they can be spread on paper toweling to absorb moisture. Sprouts will keep much better if all excess water is removed.

Store in Refrigerator

Store sprouts loosely in covered glass or plastic containers. Place folded paper toweling in the bottom of the storage container to absorb any remaining moisture. Do not use plastic bags, as the tender shoots are easily crushed or broken and the sprouts will quickly spoil.

Length of Time to Store Sprouts

For best flavor and nutrition, use sprouts as soon as they are harvest length. However, there is no need to wait, as most sprouts are delicious from the time the shoots first appear. In this case they will likely be used up by the time they are harvest length. If smaller amounts of sprouts are regularly started every two or three days, there will always be a fresh supply on hand, and there will be little or no need to store them at all. In any event, do not plan to store them more than two or three days.

Some grain sprouts such as wheat, barley and rye will continue to grow even under refrigeration, so they should be stored in the coldest part of the refrigerator and used as soon as possible.

Freezing and Drying Sprouts

Freezing is not a suitable storage method, since the shoots become soggy and limp when thawed. Grain sprouts that are going to be cooked before defrosting could be frozen, but sprouts are so inexpensive and easy to grow, that it's hardly worthwhile.

An over-supply of sprouts can be dried in a warm oven in a few hours. Whirl them in the blender for a short time and store the powder in air-tight jars. Very few nutrients are lost by drying, and this powder is very convenient to have on hand. If garbanzo or soybean sprouts are oven roasted they can be chopped or ground and used to replace nuts in many recipes. The grain sprouts—wheat, rye, triticale, and others, can be dried or roasted, ground fine and used to replace flour in baked products.

CHAPTER V

SPROUTING METHODS AND EQUIPMENT

There are several methods that can be used for sprouting seeds. They are all successful and all accomplish the same thing—they provide a warm, dark, moist environment for the growing seeds. However, each seed or group of related seeds usually needs a little different treatment to obtain the best results. Some of the most successful and commonly used methods are presented in this chapter. In Chapter VI specific recommendations are made for sprouting individual seeds. The methods described and recommended are the ones that produced best results in actual sprouting test. A little experimenting will soon determine the methods best suited for individual needs. Burlap sacks, terry cloth towels, kitchen trays and racks, etc. are sometimes used and also give satisfactory results.

Little or no expense is involved in getting started on a sprouting program, since many utensils and items commonly found in a kitchen can be used. In addition to the sprouting containers, it is convenient to have a set of measuring cups and spoons, a large colander and a large mesh strainer available.

Glass Jar Method

Equipment Needed:
Wide-Mouth Glass Jar (1-quart size)
Jar Ring to fit Jar, Rubber band or String
Circle of Plastic Screen cut to fit Jar, Cheese Cloth, Nylon Net
    or Piece of Nylon Stocking

Measure, wash and place seeds in the jar with one to two cups of warm water at 70° to 80°. Cover the top of the jar with the circle of plastic screen and secure it with the jar ring (or stretch cheese cloth, nylon net, or a nylon stocking over the jar opening and secure it with a rubber band, jar ring or string.) Leave the jar in a warm place and soak the seeds overnight or for the length of time recommended for specific seeds.

Next morning, drain the seeds and retain the soak water if it is to be used later. Rinse the seeds with cool water, then rinse them again with warm water and drain them well. Tilt the bottle on its side, mouth down, in a bowl, dish or pan so that excess water can drain away. Make certain seeds do not remain standing in water, and be sure air can circulate in the bottle. Place the jar in a warm, dark closet or cupboard or cover the bottle with dark cloth or a paper bag to keep out light.

Rinse the seeds every four to six hours during the day. If this is not possible, seeds can be successfully sprouted by rinsing morning and evening and again at bedtime. Let them stand in cool water five or ten minutes before draining in the evening to soak up plenty of water.

The glass jar is the simplest method of sprouting and the one commonly used by beginners. With the exception of gelatinous seeds, it is suitable for almost all types of seeds, beans and grains.

1. GLASS JAR METHOD—Wide-mouth jars using jar ring with plastic screen, jar ring with cheese cloth, and rubber band with nylon net. Jars containing wheat and alfalfa sprouts tilted in pan to allow for drainage. Jar of harvest-size sprouts.

Wood and Plastic Screen Tray Method

Equipment Needed:
8 x 10 x 1½ inch Wooden Tray with Plastic Window Screen
    Bottom (This size will fit in one side of double sink)
Cookie Sheets or Shallow Pans for Draining
Paper Toweling
Jar or Container for Water

Trays can often be purchased in shops or stores that carry sprouting seeds. If they are not available, it is a simple matter to make them for a few cents each. If grooves are made in the sides of the trays for a removable wooden divider, two different kinds of seeds can be sprouted at the same time.

Soak the seeds in a jar overnight or for the length of time recommended for specific seeds. Next morning, drain off the soak water and retain it if it is to be used later. Rinse the seeds and empty them into the tray. If the bottom of the tray is immersed in a pan or sink full of water, seeds can be more evenly distributed. Drain and set the tray on the rim of a cookie sheet or shallow pan so that excess water will drain from the seeds and air can circulate underneath the tray. Never set the tray on a flat surface where seeds can remain standing in water. Cover the seeds with two layers of damp paper toweling and place them in a warm, dark cupboard or closet. If several trays are to be stacked, only the top one need be covered with damp paper toweling.

Rinse the seeds every four to six hours by immersing the tray in cool water or pouring water over the seeds. If this is not possible, keep a paper towel damp by folding another paper towel to a three-inch width and putting one end of it in a container of water and the other end on the paper towel over the seeds. This will keep the seeds damp, but make sure the tray is immersed in water at least morning and evening. This will prevent mold and bacteria from multiplying and will keep the sprouts from growing through the screen.

2. *WOOD AND PLASTIC SCREEN METHOD—Soy beans soaking in jar. Two wooden trays with plastic screen bottoms stacked over drip pan. Divided wooden tray with harvest-size garbanzo sprouts. Right-hand side illustrates how to keep seeds damp with paper towels and container of water.*

Flower Pot Method

Equipment Needed:
New Unglazed Clay Flower Pot with Clay Dish
Burlap, Plastic Screen or Nylon Net
Foil Pie Plate or similar Cover
Jar Ring or Wooden Blocks
Paper Toweling

Wash the flower pot and soak it in cold water overnight. Cut a circle of plastic screen or two layers of burlap or nylon net and place them on the inside bottom of the flower pot over the opening. Pour in the soaked seeds and rinse them with warm water by holding the pot under the kitchen faucet. Drain them well. Cover the seeds with another double thickness of burlap or paper toweling which has been dampened. Cover the pot with a foil plate or other loose-fitting lid. Place a jar ring or two small wooden blocks about one inch high in the clay dish and place the flower pot on them. This allows for better drainage and circulation of air. This method provides a dark atmosphere, so the pot can be left on a kitchen cabinet if desired. Room temperature should be approximately 72°. Rinse at least three times daily by filling the pot with water and letting it drain out. Clay pots are porous and will absorb odors, so clean them thoroughly between sproutings. If sprouts have been allowed to spoil while in the clay pot, sterilize it by boiling before using it again for sprouting.

3. *FLOWER POT METHOD—Clay flower pot with clay dish and jar ring; circle of plastic screen to cover hole in flower pot. Soaked seeds are ready to go into flower pot. Damp folded paper towel and foil plate cover top and keep out light.*

Crock Method

Equipment Needed:
Earthenware Crock, Cookie Jar, Deep Stainless Steel or
     Plastic Bowl
Burlap, Terry Cloth Toweling or Paper Toweling
Plate or other Lid

This method is suitable for larger seeds and beans. Pre-soak the seeds, rinse them, and drain them well. Place the seeds in the bottom of the container and cover them with damp burlap, terry toweling, or two layers of damp paper towels. Cover the crock or container with a loose-fitting lid and, if it is not light-tight, keep it in a dark cupboard or closet. The temperature should remain at approximately 72°. Rinse the sprouts at least three times daily, and be absolutely certain that they are drained well after each rinsing. With this method there are no drain holes, and the crock or container must be tipped up and the water poured out. Seeds can be kept in the crock by holding one hand on the burlap or toweling over the sprouts. Rinse out the burlap and terry cloth toweling or change the paper towels every day. The crock method seems to keep the seeds warmer and is very satisfactory *If The Seeds Are Drained Thoroughly After Each Rinsing.*

4. *CROCK METHOD—Deep plastic bowl with soaked seeds, damp folded paper towel for covering seeds, and foil plate to keep out light. Deep stainless steel bowl and plate are also satisfactory utensils for the crock method.*

Plastic Tub Method

Equipment Needed:
Deep Plastic Container (Ice Cream or Cottage Cheese
    Containers, etc.)
Outer Container (Dark Plastic Flower Pot, Small Bucket,
    Can, etc.)
Foil Plates
Paper Toweling, Burlap or Terry Cloth
Small bag of Marbles or Rocks

Punch 1/8 inch holes in the bottom of the plastic container (a hot ice pick works very well). Presoak the seeds, rinse, drain, and place them in the bottom of sprouting container. Cover the seeds with two layers of damp paper toweling, burlap or terry cloth. For Mung beans only, place the small bag of marbles or rocks on top of the paper toweling to weight down the seeds.

The outer container should be deeper and slightly larger than the sprouting container. A dark green plastic flower pot makes an ideal outer container for a one-quart ice cream or cottage cheese carton. It allows for excellent drainage and good circulation of air. A small bucket, large can or any container large enough and deep enough for the sprouting container to fit into would serve satisfactorily, but be sure to punch large holes in the bottom, or cut it out completely, to provide drainage and circulation of air. This method works best if the sprout container fits just tight enough to hang from the top edge of the outer container and does not rest on the bottom (or use a jar ring or two small blocks of wood for the sprouting container to rest upon).

Set the outer container on a foil plate to catch drippings. Cover the top with another foil plate or loose-fitting lid. This method provides a dark interior for the sprouts, so they can be left on the kitchen cabinet if desired. Room temperature should be approximately 72°.

To rinse, remove the inside container and immerse it in and out of a pan or sink full of water several times to wash the sprouts and keep them from growing through the holes in the bottom. Drain well after each rinsing. Rinse the burlap or terry cloth each day and change paper toweling when it begins to get discolored.

5. PLASTIC TUB METHOD—White plastic ice cream carton with holes punched in the bottom for holding seeds; dark green plastic flower pot as outside container; jar ring and foil plate. Folded damp paper towel and bag of small rocks for covering seeds. Use foil plate to cover top. Also shown are large-size plastic containers for sprouting large quantities of seeds. A plate of harvest-length Mung beans are in foreground.

Sprinkle Method

Equipment Needed:
Pyrex Pie Plate or Shallow Pyrex Baking Casserole
Cheese Cloth or paper toweling
Plastic Bag

This method should always be used for gelatinous seeds. It can also be used for some of the leafy, green sprouts such as alfalfa, mustard, radish, etc. When water is added to the gelatinous seeds they form a gelatin-like mass and cannot be drained by using the other methods. Measure two tablespoons of water into a pie plate and evenly distribute one tablespoon of dry seed over the water. Do not presoak gelatinous seeds. Within an hour the seeds and water will have formed a solid jelly-like mass and will stick to the bottom of the dish. Tip the dish carefully to one side to drain off excess water. These seeds do not require much water and may be lightly sprinkled twice daily, using a spray bottle.

The following sprinkle method can be used for gelatinous seeds or for the leafy, green sprouts mentioned above. Cut two layers of cheese cloth or paper toweling to fit a plate or casserole. Fit them into the plate and sprinkle dry gelatinous seeds or presoaked other small seeds evenly over the cheese cloth or paper toweling. Sprinkle with a spray bottle to dampen the toweling and seeds. Be careful there is no excess water left in the dish. Sprinkle once or twice daily with a spray bottle to keep the seeds moist. In a day or two, after non-gelatinous sprouts have become attached to the toweling, they may be carefully flooded with cool water and drained once a day. Be very careful not to dislodge the toweling or cheese cloth from the plate.

Slip the plate into a plastic bag, leaving the end of the bag partially open for circulation of air. Keep sprouts in a warm, dark closet or cupboard or in a paper bag to shut out the light. When sprouts are about 1/4 inch long, leave them in the light to develop chlorophyll and to finish growing.

6. SPRINKLE METHOD—Pyrex plate with harvest-size garden cress. Use plastic spray bottle for applying water. Slip plate into plastic bag to retain moisture during sprouting process.

CHAPTER VI

SPECIFIC INSTRUCTIONS
FOR SPROUTING INDIVIDUAL SEEDS

Seeds that can be successfully sprouted are individually discussed in this chapter. Sprouting methods to use, sprouting time, yield, nutritive value and ways to use the sprouts are also given. Most seeds should be soaked overnight or 8 to 12 hours. Very small seeds need be soaked no longer than 2 or 3 hours. A few seeds, including gelatinous ones, should not be soaked at all. Mung beans and some of the hard beans need a longer soaking period. Specific instructions are given for individual seeds. Unless otherwise noted, the growing temperature for sprouts should be kept at approximately 72 degrees. The sprouting time given and the length of the shoot when harvested is when the sprout should be at its peak. However, sprouts may be eaten shortly after the shoot appears, and all the time they are growing to harvest length.

Adzuki Beans

Glass Jar, Crock, Tray or Flower Pot Method
Sprouting time is about 4 days or when shoot is ½ to 1 inch
long
¼ cup seed yields 1 cup sprouts

These are small red beans, common to China and Japan. They are high in protein, iron, niacin and calcium. Chop and use them in meat loaf, meat patties, combine with other vegetables or add them to vegetable soup. Steam lightly, chill and add them to salads. They should be steamed 5 to 10 minutes if used in uncooked dishes.

Alfalfa

Glass Jar, Flat Tray, or Sprinkle Method
Sprouting time is 3 to 5 days or when the shoot is 1 to
2 inches long. Leave in indirect light the last day or two
to develop the chlorophyll.
1½ Tablespoons seed makes 1 quart sprouts

Alfalfa is high in protein and the sprouts have a very high chlorophyll content when green. They are a good source of Vitamin D, E, U and the blood-clotting Vitamin K. They contain many important minerals, including iron, calcium and potassium.

Alfalfa sprouts are best eaten raw. They are especially delicious in green salads, and can be used to replace all or part of the lettuce. Substitute alfalfa sprouts for lettuce in sandwiches or tacos or as a garnish instead of parsley. Blend them in fruit or vegetable juices for a refreshing, vitamin-packed drink. They may be used in jellied salads, omelets, soups, fritters or potato pancakes. For baking, harvest the sprout when it is no more than ¼ inch long and add to breads, cookies and muffins.

Almonds

Glass Jar or Tray Method
Soak almonds 18 hours before sprouting
Sprouting time is 3 or 4 days or when the shoot is ¼ inch long
1 cup almonds yields 1½ cups sprouts

Almonds are approximately 18% protein and are a good source of calcium and potassium. They may be used chopped in ice cream, cookies, salads, for almond milk, milk shakes, candy or any recipe that calls for unsprouted almonds. They can be eaten plain as any other nut.

Barley

Glass Jar or Flower Pot Method
Sprouting time is 3 or 4 days or when shoot is length of seed
½ cup seed makes 1 cups sprouts

Barley is about 10% protein and contains calcium, phosphorus and potassium in significant amounts. Add barley sprouts to salads, soups and cereals. They may be ground and added to pancake or waffle batter or to muffins and quick breads.

Bean Group (Black, Kidney, Lima, Navy, Pinto, Red, White, or any Hard Bean)

Tray, Flower Pot, Tub or Jar Method
Sprouting time is 2 to 3 days or when the shoot is ¼ to ½ inch long. Do not sprout over 3 days or let the shoot get longer than ½ inch.
1 cup beans will yield 4 cups of sprouts

Beans are easily sprouted, but care must be taken to keep them rinsed well so that they will not decay. The tray method works best, since there aren't too many layers of beans and better air circulation.

Beans contain from 20 to 25% protein, and are the best source of vegetable protein. They also contain appreciable amounts of calcium, iron, niacin, phosphorus, potassium, Vitamins B1 and B2. Sprouting eliminates the gas-producing qualities found in beans. They should be cooked or steamed before eating. Each type bean has a different flavor, but they may be combined and cooked together for an interesting and unusual taste treat. Always cook beans on low heat in plain water with no salt or seasoning until they are tender.

Grind the sprouted beans and add them to meat or vegetable patties and loaves. Steam, chill and add them to salads, mash and use them alone or in combination with meat, fish or cheese for sandwich spreads. They are a good addition to soups and casseroles and can be mashed and used in baking. Use sprouted beans in chili, baked beans, tamale pie or any recipe where unsprouted beans are used. Not only will sprouting decrease the cooking time and increase the quantity of beans, but they taste much more delicious than unsprouted beans.

Chia Seeds

Sprinkle Method
Sprouting time is 4 to 6 days or when 1½ to 2 inches long
When sprouts are ¼ inch long leave in indirect light to green
1 Tablespoon yields 2 cups sprouts

Chia seeds are well-known by the Indians of the American Southwest and Mexico. The seeds gave them strength and endurance and were sometimes the only food they had for days at a time on long hunting expeditions. They are rich in calcium, copper, iron, iodine, magnesium, phosophorus and are a good source of protein and vegetable fat.

Chia sprouts have a tangy taste and add variety and spice to salads, soups, spreads, dips, sandwiches and appetizers. They are best used raw or added to soups just before serving.

Clover (Red)

Glass Jar, Flower Pot or Tray Method
Sprouting time is 3 to 5 days or when shoot is 1 to 2 inches
    long
When the shoot is ½ inch long, place in indirect light to green
1½ Tablespoon of seed yields about 1 quart of sprouts

Red clover sprouts are similar to alfalfa sprouts. When greened, they have a high chlorophyll content. They also contain important minerals and vitamins.

These sprouts are best eaten raw, and are a delicious addition to green salads. Clover sprouts can replace lettuce in sandwiches or tacos. Use them in any recipe that calls for alfalfa sprouts.

Corn

Glass Jar, Flower Pot or Tray Method
Sprouting time is 3 or 4 days or when the shoot is no more
    than ¾ inch
1 cup seed will yield 2 cups sprouts

Corn does not contain a complete protein, but when eaten at the same meal with beans or other seeds, they can together form a complete protein. It contains Vitamin A, potassium and phosphorus.

Corn sprouts have an enjoyable sweet taste and can be steamed and served as a vegetable. They are good in casseroles, tamale pie, soups and stews. If the sprouts are dried and ground they are satisfactory to use as cornmeal for muffins, breads and cereals.

Cress (Garden)

Sprinkle Method
Sprouting time is 4 or 5 days or when shoot is 1 to 1½
    inches long

When sprout is ¼ inch long, place in indirect light to green
1 Tablespoon seed yields 1½ cups sprouts

Cress is a gelatinous seed and must not be soaked. Sprinkle the dry seed directly on to the damp plate or cheese cloth and keep moist with sprinkling.

Cress is extremely high in Vitamin A and C. The sprouts have a peppery taste and are very good in vegetable salads, sandwiches, sour cream and yogurt dips and appetizers. Because of their spicy flavor, only a few sprouts are needed to give a tangy taste to dishes. They can be used in place of chives or parsley for garnishes.

Fenugreek

Glass Jar, Tray, Plastic Tub or Flower Pot Method
Sprouting time is 3 to 4 days or when sprout is ½ to 1 inch
   long
¼ cup seed will yield 1 cups sprouts

Do not sprout these seeds too long or they will become bitter. They are high in protein, Vitamin A, iron and choline. Fenugreek has long been used in the Far East for making curry powder, and tea made from the seeds is used for medicinal purposes. The soak water can be saved and used as a tea.

Fenugreek sprouts are spicy, but if sprouted over 3 or 4 days they become bitter. They add flavor to curry dishes, cream sauces, dips and salads. Stir into soup just before serving, but do not cook them.

Flax Seeds

Sprinkle Method
Sprouting time is 3 or 4 days or when sprout is about
   1 inch long
When sprout is ¼ inch long, place in indirect light
2 Tablespoons seed yields about 2 cups sprouts

Flax is a gelatinous seed and must not be soaked. Sprinkle the dry seed directly on to the damp plate or cheese cloth and keep moist with sprinkling. Flax seed contains an appreciable amount of protein, niacin, iron and calcium.

Flax seed sprouts have a mild flavor and can be substituted for lettuce in sandwiches or salads. Add them to soup or cereal at the last minute, but do not cook them.

Garbanzo (Chickpea)

Tray or Glass Jar Method
Sprouting time is 3 or 4 days or when sprout is ½ inch long
1 cup seed yields about 3 cups sprouts

Water must be changed two or three times during the soaking period. They should be rinsed 4 to 6 times in a 24 hour period, as they sour quickly when wet.

Garbanzo sprouts are approximately 20% protein. They contain iron, and are a good source of Vitamin A and C.

Garbanzo sprouts may be steamed and served with butter as a vegetable. Add them to soups, salads, sandwich spreads, casseroles, vegetable and meat loaves, etc. They should always be steamed or cooked before using in uncooked dishes. They can be oven-roasted and used as a substitute for nuts in many recipes.

Lentils

Glass Jar or Tray Method
Sprouting time is 3 or 4 days. They can be used when the
  shoot is the length of the seed or up to 1 inch in length.
¼ cup seed yields about 2 cups of sprouts

Lentils are mentioned in the Bible and are one of the oldest vegetables known to man. There are many varieties of lentils, but the small brown ones are best for sprouting. They contain approximately 24% protein as well as Vitamin C, Vitamin E, iron, phosphorus and potassium.

Lentil sprouts have a tangy, peppery taste, and add a delicious flavor to green salads. They can be steamed a few minutes, buttered and served as a vegetable. They are especially good in soups, stews, main dishes or wherever unsprouted lentils are used.

Millet

Glass Jar Method
Sprouting Time is 3 or 4 days or when shoot is ¼ inch long
½ cup seed makes 1 cup sprouts

Millet is a small cereal grain rich in iron and niacin. It contains nearly 10% protein as well as phosphorus and Vitamin B2.

It is very easily digested, making it suitable for children, babies and elderly people on bland diets.

Millet sprouts have a sweet flavor similar to corn. They may be cooked as a vegetable or breakfast cereal. Sprouts may be added to soups and casseroles or used in breads and muffins.

Mung Beans

Plastic Tub, Glass Jar, or Crock Method

Sprouting time is 2 to 5 days. Sprouts may be used when ¼ to 2 inches in length, or grown to 3-inch commercial size.

¼ cup seed yields about 3 to 4 cups sprouts

Wash mung beans in very warm water and soak 12 to 18 hours. Change water several times during soak period. Rinse often while sprouting to insure a sweet flavor and prevent decay. The plastic tub method with a weight of small rocks or marbles will produce thicker, more tender sprouts. Be sure that sprouts are drained well after each rinsing.

Mung beans are the best known and most popular of the sprouting seeds. They have been a staple in Oriental diets for centuries. Mung beans are 24% protein, and the sprouts are a good source of choline, calcium, iron, Vitamin A and E.

The hull has a slightly bitter taste and most people prefer to remove it before eating the sprout, although many don't bother. The sprouts are a crunchy addition to salads of all kinds—green, potato and gelatin. They are used in Oriental dishes, fried rice, casseroles, soups and dips. They make a delicious vegetable if barely heated and served with butter.

Mustard (Black)

Glass Jar or Sprinkle Method

Sprouting time is 3 or 4 days or when the shoot is 1 to 1½ inches in length. When shoot is ¼ inch long, place in indirect light.

2 Tablespoons seed will yield about 3 cups sprouts

Mustard sprouts are a good source of chlorophyll, Vitamins A and C, phosphorus, iron, niacin and potassium.

The sprouts have a spicy taste and add zest to green salads, dips and appetizers. They may be added to soups just before serving.

Oats

> Sprinkle Method with paper towel
> Sprouting time is 3 or 4 days or when shoot is length of
> seed
> 1 cup seed yields 2½ cups sprouts

Do not presoak oats. Place two layers of paper toweling in pyrex baking dish. Spray to dampen towel and sprinkle oats in a thin layer on the towel. Use a plastic spray bottle to spray them once a day and keep them barely moist. Slip the container into a plastic bag, leaving one end partially open for ventilation.

Oats are 14% protein and are rich in Vitamin B1. They also contain other B Vitamins and Vitamin E. They are a good source of iron, zinc and other minerals.

The oat sprouts can be used as a breakfast cereal or as a buttered vegetable. They are a good substitute for any of the other grain sprouts in breads, soups and main dishes.

Peas

> Flat Tray, Glass Jar or Flower Pot Methods
> Sprouting time is 3 to 4 days or when shoot is length of
> seed
> 1 cup of seed makes about 2 cups of sprouts

There are many varieties of peas, but the Alaskan Pea is considered very good for sprouting. Peas are about 22% protein and contain all eight essential amino acids. After sprouting, they taste similar to fresh peas. They become tougher as the sprout grows longer, and are much better if eaten when the sprout is no longer than the seed itself.

Peas sprouts may be used in soups, as a fresh vegetable, ground for use in vegetable or meat loaves and patties. Use them in any recipe calling for fresh or dried peas. Sprouted peas should be lightly steamed and chilled before adding to salads, spreads, relishes or any uncooked dishes.

Pumpkin Seeds

> Glass Jar Method
> Sprouting time is 3 or 4 days or when shoot is barely
> showing and no longer than ¼ inch.
> 1 cup seed yields about 2 cups sprouts

Pumpkin seeds are high in protein, iron and the B Vitamins. They are sometimes sold in small packages as a snack food as are sunflower seeds.

After sprouting they can be eaten raw or lightly toasted to eat as a snack. They can be chopped and added to breads, candy and desserts.

Radish Seed

Glass Jar or Sprinkle Method with paper toweling
Sprouting time is 2 to 4 days or when the shoot is 1½ to 2 inches.
When shoot is ¼ inch long, place in indirect light to green
1 Tablespoon seed yields about 2 cups of sprouts

Radish sprouts have a strong radish flavor. They become hot as they get older, or if they do not get enough water. They are rich in vitamins and minerals.

Use radish sprouts to give a zesty flavor to green salad. Sprinkle them on cottage cheese or yogurt or add them to soup just before serving. They are best if eaten raw.

Rice

Glass Jar or Tray Method
Sprouting time is 3 or 4 days or when shoot is length of seed
1 cup of rice yields 2½ cups of sprouts

Brown rice contains only about 7% protein, but contains all eight essential amino acids. It is a good source of Niacin and Vitamins C and E.

Rice sprouts are bland in flavor and combine well with other foods. They are good in soups, cereals, breads, main dishes or any recipe using unsprouted rice.

Rye

Glass Jar, Tray or Tub Method
Sprouting time is about 2 days or when shoot is length of grain.
Temperature for sprouting should be cooler than most sprouts—no more than 68°.
1 cup of rye yields 3 cups of sprouts

Rye is 12% protein and is rich in iron, potassium, phosphorus, manganese and Vitamin E.

Rye sprouts are similar to wheat sprouts, but more mild, and are delicious when eaten raw as a snack. They can be used in soups, cereal casseroles and main dishes. Rye sprouts combine well with sprouted rice dishes and are a good addition to steamed puddings, vegetables, jellied fruit and vegetable salads, cookies and baked products. They make an excellent sprouted rye bread. For baking, do not allow the shoot to grow longer than the grain itself, or the bread may be sticky. For green salads, the grain may be sprouted one more day.

Sesame Seeds

Glass Jar Method

Sprouting time is 2 or 3 days or until the shoot barely shows. If allowed to grow longer it will become bitter.

½ cup seed yields 1 cup sprouts. Use only unhulled seeds for sprouting

Sesame seeds are a valuable source of protein, and are extremely high in calcium. They also contain Vitamin B1, niacin, lecithin, and Vitamins A and E. Sesame seed sprouts are delicious blended in milk shakes, malts and other drinks. Toast them lightly and use in breads, desserts, candies, and sprinkle them on salads and scrambled eggs. The sprouts can be used in any recipe that calls for unsprouted sesame seeds.

Soybeans

Tray, Glass Jar or Flower Pot Method

Sprouting time is 3 or 4 days or until the shoot is ¼ to 1 inch long. They must be rinsed 4 to 6 times a day to prevent souring.

Soak them about 12 hours and change the water 3 or 4 times.

1 cup seed yields 3 to 4 cups sprouts

Soybeans are the most nutritious of all beans. They contain from 33% to 40% protein, and can be used as a meat substitute. They are rich in the B Vitamins, lecithin, Vitamins A and E, iron and calcium. One half cup of the sprouts contain as much Vitamin C as six glasses of orange juice.

Soybean sprouts can be eaten raw, but most people prefer to steam lightly and chill them before adding to salads or un-cooked dishes. Grind soybean sprouts and add to egg dishes, casseroles, stuffings for poultry, vegetable or meat loaves and patties or stews. Use them for Chili, in Oriental dishes, soups, aspice and vegetarian dishes. Blend them in vegetable juices for a nutritious drink. If the sprouts are oven roasted and ground, they may be substituted for nuts in many recipes.

Sunflower Seeds

Glass Jar Method
Sprouting time is about 3 days or until the shoot barely appears
They become bitter if allowed to grow longer
Temperature should be about 80° for best results in sprouting
½ cup seed yields 1 cup sprouts
Unhulled seeds are more often used for sprouting, but some of the hulled ones can be used. Check with the supplier to be sure of good quality seed.

Sunflower seeds are about 30% protein. They contain unsaturated oils, calcium, iron and Vitamins D and E.

Sunflower seed sprouts make excellent snacks. They are delicious when added to salads, cookies, nut breads and muffins. Toast them lightly before using for the best flavor.

Triticale

Glass Jar or Tray Method
Sprouting time is 2 or 3 days or when shoot is seed length
1 cup seed yields 2 cups sprouts

Triticale is a cross between wheat and rye and is slightly higher in protein—about 14%. It contains B Vitamins, Vitamins C and E, and some of the trace minerals.

The sprouts can be used in soups, salads, cereals, casseroles and in recipes using rye and wheat sprouts.

Wheat

Glass Jar or Tray Method
Sprouting time is about 24 hours or when shoot is 1/8 inch

long for baking. Sprout one more day for use in salads.
1 cup wheat will yield 2 to 3 cups sprouts

Wheat is about 12% protein and contains Vitamin E and niacin. After sprouting, the Vitamin C content is greatly increased, as are the other vitamins and minerals.

Wheat sprouts can be used in many ways—bread, pancakes, cookies, cakes, cereals, puddings, stews, meat loaves and patties, chili, soups and salads. Sprouted wheat makes a very delicious yeast bread. Be sure that the shoot is no longer than 1/8 inch or the bread may be sticky. Sprout one more day for salads. If allowed to get longer than the grain the sprouts develop a sweet taste.

Miscellaneous Vegetable Seeds (Cabbage, Cauliflower, Broccoli, Brussels Sprouts, Turnips, Beets, Chard, Endive, Lettuce, Etc.)

Glass Jar Method
Sprouting time is 3 to 5 days or when sprout is 1 or 2
    inches long
Leave in indirect light the last day to green sprouts

One tablespoon of seed will yield approximately 2 cups of sprouts, depending on the type of seed.

Vegetable sprouts are a good source of iron, potassium, phosphorus, niacin, Vitamin A and C and other minerals and vitamins.

They are a delicious addition to salads, sandwiches, or for a garnish for appetizers, cottage cheese, yogurt and eggs.

CHAPTER VII

DEHYDRATED FOODS AND SPROUTS—
HOME STORAGE PROGRAMS

Sprouts Supplement Dehydrated Foods

Every home storage program should contain seeds for sprouting. There are many ways in which sprouts can be used to supplement dehydrated, dried, canned or freeze-dried products. A family could maintain excellent health during a time of emergency by combining these basic storage items with sprouts. Seeds, beans and grains can be sprouted and fresh produce will be available any time of the year in two to six days. They are highly compatible with dehydrated and dried foods, and can be added or combined with recipes to enhance and give variety to the diet. Since the maximum benefit is obtained from sprouts by eating them fresh, there is no need to worry about cooking facilities in times of an extremely dire disaster. There is no food spoilage or waste, as seeds can be sprouted as needed.

Sprouts Insure Better Health

If fresh vegetables were not available for a prolonged period of time, the vitamins, minerals, enzymes and proteins contained in sprouts could very well mean the difference between health and illness, or in some cases, perhaps even between life and death. The basic storage items are not a source of enzymes which control the chemical reactions in the body so necessary for good health. These enzymes must be replaced in the body by eating fresh garden produce. Seeds, grains and beans which have been sprouted contain these enzymes, and are a dependable way to replenish them. Therefore, sprouting seeds can supply an important part of the diet, which may not otherwise be available in an emergency.

For elderly people, invalids, babies or small children and those on smooth or bland diets, it could be a shock to the system to suddenly have only wheat, beans, grains or other roughage. However, after sprouting, the composition of these same items is drastically changed. Sprouts contain as much as 95% water, and are much more easily broken down and assimilated by the body. Many of the sprouts can be prepared to provide suitable foods for those needing special diets. For instance soybeans, almonds and sunflower seeds can be used to make a delicious, highly nutritious milk.

Buying Seeds for Storage

In many cases the grains and beans normally used for the home storage or emergency programs can be sprouted. If they have been stored for several years or have been treated in such a way that the germ has been killed, then they will not be viable. It would be wise to check the supply to see if stored wheat, rice, beans, grains, etc. will sprout. If so, then a variety of other seed for sprouting can be added to those already on hand.

Some seeds will germinate after several years, if they are sealed from moisture and stored in a cool, dark place. On the other hand, many seeds have a very low percent of viability after the first year. This is especially true of soybeans. In most cases maximum germination for seeds will be obtained from the current year's crop. When purchasing sprouting seeds, read the labels on packages, select a reliable supplier who will guarantee his product and do not buy more than will be used in one year. Always rotate to keep the supply fresh, using the oldest ones first. Store the seeds in air-tight bottles, plastic containers or cans and label them showing quantity, variety and date of purchase.

Amounts of Seeds Needed for Storage

The amount of seeds stored for sprouting will vary depending on individual tastes and preferences. The suggested types and amounts of seeds recommended for storage are for a few of the well-known and best-enjoyed sprouts. Others may be added or substituted, depending on individual preferences. Before storing seeds for sprouting, it would be wise to buy small packages of several varieties and sprout them. Then determine which ones are best liked by the family. There is no point in storing seeds or anything else that will not be eaten. If sprouts are already being used in the diet, a family will not have to become accustomed to something new in an emergency.

The seeds recommended for storage and sprouting will provide an abundance of all vitamins, minerals and amino acids needed by the body. They are excellent sources of protein as well. While it is not suggested that sprouts be used exclusively for emergencies, it can be done. There is a family in Utah who survived on sprouts for six months during the winter and maintained excellent health.

The following amounts recommended for storage are for one adult for one year, to be used to supplement dehydrated, dried, canned or other storage foods. If a larger variety of storage seeds are desired, then these amounts could be decreased accordingly. Remember that sprouting increases the volume of the seeds. When sprouted, wheat will at least double in volume and some of the other seeds will increase much more than that. Also, decrease amounts if there are several small children involved. These are merely suggested amounts, and should be adjusted according to individual family needs.

Amount to Store for One Adult for One Year

Type of Seed	Amount
Alfalfa Seed	6 pounds
Pinto or other beans	15 pounds
Lentils	6 pounds
Mung Beans	6 pounds
Peas (Alaskan)	10 pounds
Rye	10 pounds
Soybeans	15 pounds
Wheat (Sprouting)	25 pounds

Sprouting Recipes for all seasons

CHAPTER VIII

RECIPES FOR APPETIZERS

Cheesy Wheat Balls

1/2 cup wheat sprouts, chopped
1/4 tsp onion salt

4 oz. cream cheese
2 oz. blue cheese
1/2 cup walnuts, finely chopped

Soften cream cheese at room temperature and blend in wheat sprouts, onion salt and crumbled blue cheese. Mix well and roll into 1-inch balls. Roll in the chopped nuts and chill before serving. 18 balls.

Armenian Sprout Dip

1/4 cup lentil sprouts
1/4 cup alfalfa sprouts
3 Tbsp minced green onion
1 tsp wine vinegar

1/4 cup mung sprouts
1 cup yogurt
1/4 tsp salt
twist ground black pepper

Chop the sprouts and blend in the seasonings. Fold into the yogurt and chill two hours to blend flavors. Serve with raw vegetable slices, crackers or chips. Makes 1½ cups.

Tuna Sprout Spread

1/2 cup mung bean sprouts
1 Tbsp finely chopped onion
2 Tbsp yogurt
1/8 tsp salt

1/2 cup tuna fish, canned
2 Tbsp minced celery
1 Tbsp lemon juice
twist ground black pepper

Chop the mung bean sprouts and combine with remaining ingredients. Chill one hour before serving. Spread on toast rounds, crackers, or serve with cucumber slices, carrot rounds and turnip slices. Makes 1 cup.

Alfa-Cheese Dip

1 cup Alfalfa sprouts	4 oz. cream cheese
4 Tbsp yogurt	4 Tbsp mayonnaise
2 Tbsp minced chives	1/2 tsp celery seed
1/2 tsp salt	twist ground black pepper

Chop alfalfa sprouts fine. Soften cream cheese at room temperature. Blend sprouts into softened cheese and stir in the yogurt and mayonnaise, and add the seasonings. Mix well and chill before serving. Serve with crackers, chips or crisp vegetable slices or sticks. Makes 1½ cups.

Sprouts and Avocado Dip

1/2 cup mung bean sprouts	1/2 cup lentil sprouts
1 large avocado	2 Tbsp mayonnaise
2 Tbsp yogurt	2 Tbsp crumbled bacon or
1 tsp lemon juice	bacon sprout bits
1/8 tsp salt	twist ground black pepper

Peel and mash avocado and add lemon juice, mayonnaise, yogurt, bacon, salt and pepper. Chop the sprouts very fine and fold into the avocado mixture. Chill well and serve with crackers, chips and crisp vegetable slices and sticks. Makes 1½ cups.

Bacon Sprout Bits

2 cups sprouts (soybean, garbanzo or Alaskan pea) (1/8-1/4 inch sprout)
4 Tbsp bacon drippings

Dry sprouts between layers of paper toweling and chop into medium fine pieces. Fry in bacon drippings, stirring until golden brown and crisp. Drain on brown paper. When cool, store in covered jar in refrigerator. Use for flavoring scrambled eggs. salads, dips or any recipe calling for bacon bits or bacon chips. Makes 2 cups.

Sprout Nuts (For Baking & Cooking)

2 cups sprouts (soybean, garbanzo or Alaskan pea) (1/4 inch sprout)

Dry sprouts between paper towels and arrange on baking sheets in a single layer. Bake in 350° oven 25 or 30 minutes until light golden brown. Cool and store in air tight jars. Use as a replacement for nuts in baking and cooking. Also use them in all recipes calling for oven-dried or roasted sprouts. Makes 2 cups.

Sprout Nut Snacks

2 cups sprouts (soybean, garbanzo or Alaskan pea) (1/4 inch sprout)
2 Tbsp cooking oil

1/4 tsp salt

Dry sprouts between paper towels. Evenly distribute the oil on a baking sheet. Spread the sprouts on the baking sheet in a single layer and shake baking sheet to coat the sprouts with oil. Bake in 350° oven 30 minutes until sprouts are a light golden brown. Shake pan or stir sprouts two or three times during baking. Remove from oven and sprinkle with salt. Cool before serving. Store in covered jar. Makes 2 cups.

Variations: Sprinkle with barbecue salt, season salt or a mixture of garlic, celery and onion salt.

Cucumber Sprout Spread

1/2 cup fenugreek sprouts
 (or mung bean sprouts)
1/2 cup grated cucumber
1 Tbsp minced chives
2 Tbsp chopped ripe olives
Celery

4 oz. cream cheese
2 oz. Blue cheese, crumbled
1/8 tsp salt
twist ground black pepper
Paprika

Soften cream cheese at room temperature. Chop fenugreek sprouts until very fine and add to softened cheese. Stir in drained cucumber, blue cheese, olives and salt and pepper. Use as a filling for crisp celery and sprinkle with paprika. Makes 1½ cups.

Variation: Use as a spread on crackers or as a sandwhich filling, using whole wheat bread and alfalfa sprouts.

Mushroom and Sprout Dip

3/4 cup mung bean sprouts   1/4 cup mushroom stems
1/4 cup sour cream   and pieces
2 Tbsp minced chives   1/4 cup yogurt
1/8 tsp paprika   1/8 tsp salt
twist ground black pepper

Chop mung bean sprouts very fine. Drain mushrooms and chop very fine. Combine with remaining ingredients and chill well. Serve with crisp vegetable sticks or slices, crackers, or chips. Makes 1½ cups.

Soy Peanut Butter

1 cup soy sprout nuts   1 cup raw peanuts
1/2 cup soy oil   1/4 tsp salt

Place raw peanuts on baking sheet in single layer and bake in 350° oven for 20 to 25 minutes. Cool and blend until fine in blender. Empty into bowl and blend soy sprouts nuts until fine, but not powdered. Add to blended peanuts and mix with salt and enough soy oil to make it the consistency of peanut butter. If desired, peanuts and soy sprout nuts may be more coarsely chopped for chunky butter. Makes 1½ cups.

Curried Deviled Eggs

6 hard-cooked eggs   1/2 cup mung bean sprouts
1 tsp prepared mustard   1 Tbsp mayonnaise
1/2 tsp curry powder   1/2 tsp Worcestershire sauce
1/4 tsp salt   1/8 tsp ground black pepper
2 Tbsp green alfalfa sprouts   paprika

Chop mung bean sprouts very fine. Cut eggs in half lengthwise and remove yolks and mash fine. Add remaining ingredients, except alfalfa sprouts and paprika. Mix well and stuff egg whites with mixture. Sprinkle with paprika and garnish with alfalfa sprouts, which have been chopped. Makes 12 egg halves.

Mustard Deviled Eggs

6 hard-cooked eggs
1/4 cup mustard sprouts
1/8 tsp ground black pepper
paprika

2 Tbsp mayonnaise
1/4 tsp salt
1/2 tsp prepared mustard
2 Tbsp Cress sprouts

Cut eggs in half length-wise, remove yolks and mash smooth with fork. Blend in mayonnaise, mustard, salt and pepper. Chop the mustard sprouts fine and stir into mixture. Fill egg whites with mixture, sprinkle with paprika and garnish with chopped cress sprouts. Makes 12 egg halves.

Dilled Garbanzo Sprouts

2 cups garbanzo sprouts
1/4 cup sliced onion
1 small clove garlic
1 sprig dill, fresh or dried
1 tsp sugar

1/2 cup vinegar
1/2 cup water
1 small hot red pepper.
 dried
1/2 tsp salt

Place sprouts, onion, garlic, dill weed in quart jar. Combine vinegar, water, sugar and salt. Bring to boil and stir to dissolve sugar and salt. Pour hot liquid over sprouts in jar. Cover and let cool, then refrigerate for at least 24 hours. Drain and serve cold. Makes 2 cups.

Avocado-Sprout Spread

3/4 cup alfalfa sprouts
1 Tbsp lemon juice
1 Tbsp mayonnaise
twist ground black pepper

1 medium avocado
1 tsp minced green onion
1/8 tsp salt
paprika

Peel and mash avocado and stir in lemon juice, mayonnaise, green onion and salt and pepper. Chop alfalfa sprouts fine and add. Use as a spread for toast rounds and cucumber slices. Sprinkle with paprika. Makes 1 cup.

Sprouted Wheat Balls

1 cup wheat sprouts
1/2 cup soy sprout nuts

1/2 cup finely chopped
 onion

1 beaten egg	1/2 cup wheat bread
1/2 tsp salt	crumbs
1/4 cup milk	1/8 tsp pepper
oil for frying	

Grind wheat sprouts and toasted soy sprouts. Combine with remaining ingredients and mix thoroughly. Form into 1-inch balls and fry in hot oil for about 1 minute or until golden brown. Drain on paper toweling and insert a toothpick in each one and serve hot. Makes about 18 balls.

Lentil-Clam Dip

8 oz. cream cheese	1 cup chopped lentil sprouts
2 Tbsp Worcestershire	1 Tbsp lemon juice
sauce	2 drops Tabasco sauce
1/8 tsp garlic salt	twist ground black pepper
8 oz. can minced clams	1/4 cup clam broth

Soften cream cheese at room temperature and add seasonings. Add clam juice to make it dipping consistency. Whip with fork until smooth and fluffy. Stir in clams and sprouts. Chill and serve with raw crisp vegetables, chips or crackers. Makes 2 cups.

Lentil-Onion Dip

8 oz. cream cheese	1/4 cup mayonnaise
1/2 cup yogurt	1 tsp lemon juice
1 cup lentil sprouts	
1 pkg. (1-1/2 oz.) dry onion	
soup mix	

Soften cream cheese at room temperature and combine with yogurt, mayonnaise, and soup mix. Whip with fork until light and fluffy. Stir in lemon juice and sprouts, which have been finely chopped. Chill one or two hours before serving. Serve with crisp vegetables, crackers or chips. Makes 2 cups.

Cottage Cheese Alfalfa Dip

| 1 cup alfalfa sprouts, | 1 cup creamed cottage |
| chopped | cheese |

1/4 cup milk
1/4 tsp salt
1 Tbsp chopped chives

1 Tbsp lemon juice
1/8 tsp garlic salt

Blend cottage cheese, milk, lemon juice, salt and garlic salt in blender until smooth. Stir in chives and alfalfa sprouts and chill until serving time. Serve with crisp vegetable sticks or slices. Also delicious on baked potatoes. Makes 2 cups.

Pineapple Mung Dip

1 cup chopped mung bean
   sprouts
3 oz. cream cheese

4-1/2 oz. can deviled
   ham
3/4 cup crushed pineapple

Drain pineapple reserving juice. Mix softened cream cheese, deviled ham and crushed pineapple together, adding just enough pineapple juice for dip consistency. Stir in mung bean sprouts. Chill several hours to blend flavors. Let stand at room temperature a few minutes before serving time. Serve with crisp vegetables, crackers or chips. Makes 2 cups.

Snappy Alfa-Cheese Dip

1 cup chopped alfalfa
   sprouts
1/4 cup mayonnaise
2 Tbsp grated onion
1 tsp sharp prepared mustard
1/8 tsp garlic salt

2 cups grated cheddar
   cheese
2 Tbsp chopped sweet pickle
3 Tbsp pickle juice
1/2 cup yogurt
twist black pepper

Combine cheese, mayonnaise, yogurt and pickle juice and whip with fork until smooth. Stir in seasonings and sprouts and blend well. Chill until serving time. Serve with crisp vegetables, crackers or chips. Makes 2 cups.

Dilly Mung Dip

1 cup mung bean sprouts
2 chicken bouillon cubes
1 tsp minced onion
1 Tbsp minced pimiento

8 oz. cream cheese
2 Tbsp dill pickle liquid
2 tsp lemon juice
1/4 tsp dried dill weed

Soften cream cheese at room temperature. Crush bouillon cubes in dill pickle liquid. Gradually add the bouillon to the cream cheese, beating until smooth. Stir in remaining ingredients and chill 2 hours before serving. Serve with vegetable slices or sticks, chips or crackers. Makes 2 cups.

Soy Bacon Dip

1 cup commercial sour cream	1/2 cup bacon soy sprout bits
2 Tbsp mayonnaise	1/2 cup yogurt
1/2 tsp Beau Monde seasoning	1 tsp dill weed
	1 tsp horse radish
1/8 tsp salt	twist ground black pepper
1/8 tsp garlic salt	1/8 tsp onion salt

Combine all ingredients and chill for 3 hours before serving. Serve with crackers, chips or crisp vegetables. Makes 2 cups.

Mustard Cheese Butter

1/2 cup soft butter	1/4 cup chopped mustard sprouts
1/8 tsp dry mustard	Paprika
1/4 cup chopped alfalfa sprouts	
1 cup finely grated Swiss cheese	

Stir cheese and mustard into soft butter and blend well. Add the alfalfa and mustard sprouts and blend well. Turn into serving container and sprinkle with paprika. Makes 1-1/2 cups. Serve with rye crisps.

Soy Cheese Ball

1 cup soy sprout nuts	1/2 cup crushed pineapple, drained
1 Tbsp minced onion	1 tsp seasoned salt
8 oz. cream cheese	
2 Tbsp minced green pepper	

Soften cream cheese at room temperature. Chop soy sprout nuts and add half to the cheese. Stir in remaining ingredients.

Chill for one hour and form into ball. Roll in remaining 1/2 cup finely chopped soy sprout nuts. Chill at least two hours before serving with crisp vegetables, crackers or chips.

Variation: Makes delicious sandwich spread with brown bread and alfalfa sprouts. Makes 1-1/2 cups.

Olive Cheese Ball

4 oz. cream cheese	4 oz. blue cheese
2 Tbsp soft butter	1/4 cup chopped olives
3/4 cup soy sprout nuts, finely chopped	1 tsp minced chives

Soften cheese at room temperature and combine with 1/2 cup soy nuts and remaining ingredients. Chill slightly and form into ball. Roll in remaining 1/4 cup soy nuts. Chill 2 hours. Serve with crisp vegetables, crackers or chips. Makes 1-1/4 cups.

CHAPTER IX

RECIPES FOR BEVERAGES

Low-Cal Sprout Drink

1 envelope unflavored gelatin	1 Tbsp lemon juice
	3/4 cup tomato juice
1/2 cup alfalfa sprouts	1 tsp soy sauce

Pour tomato juice into blender and add other ingredients. Blend about 30 seconds. Pour into a glass and drink at once. Makes 1 cup.

Alfa-Orange Julius

1 cup alfalfa sprouts	1/3 cup dry powdered
3 cups orange juice	skim milk
6 ice cubes, cracked	1/2 tsp vanilla

Place all ingredients in blender and process at high speed a minute or two until mixture is smooth and foamy. Serve at once. Makes 4 servings.

Alfa-Peach Julius

1 cup alfalfa sprouts	1-1/2 cups sliced, sweetened
1/2 tsp nutmeg	fresh peaches (or frozen)
2 cups milk	

Place 2 cups milk and remaining ingredients in blender. Blend at high speed a minute or two until smooth. Add remaining cup of milk and blend another few seconds. Serve at once. Makes 4 servings.

Hot Tomato-Lentil Cocktail

1 cup lentil sprouts	3 cups tomato juice
1 cup canned consomme	2 Tbsp chopped green onion

2 Tbsp minced celery	1 tsp Worcestershire sauce
1 Tbsp lemon juice	dash Tabasco sauce

Blend lentil sprouts, 1 cup tomato juice, green onion, and celery until smooth. Add remaining ingredients, heat and serve hot. Makes 4 servings.

Almond Milk

3/4 cup sprouted almonds	2 cups cold water
1 Tbsp honey	1 cup pineapple juice

Blend almonds, honey and water on high speed for 2 or 3 minutes or until smooth. Strain through coarse strainer and add pineapple juice. Serve chilled. Makes 4 servings.

Sesame Seed Milk

1 cup sprouted sesame seeds	3 cups cold water
1 Tbsp honey	1/4 tsp vanilla
1/2 cup shredded fresh coconut	

Blend 2 cups cold water, sesame seed sprouts, honey and coconut on high speed for 2 or 3 minutes or until smooth. Strain through coarse strainer and add remaining cup water and vanilla. Stir to blend and serve cold. Makes 4 servings.

Variation: Substitute sunflower seed sprouts for sesame seed sprouts.

Sprouted Soybean Milk

1-1/2 cups soybean sprouts	2 cups hot water
(1/4 inch)	2 cups warm water

Blend sprouts and 2 cups warm water in blender for 4 or 5 minutes until finely chopped. Pour into double boiler and add hot water. Cook in double boiler over boiling water for 40 minutes, stirring occasionally. Strain through strainer and store in covered container in refrigerator. This milk may be used in any recipe calling for regular milk. If it is to be served as a beverage, honey may be added if desired. The remaining pulp can be used in vegetable or meat patties or loaves. Makes 1 quart soy milk.

Soy Date Shake

Freeze 1-1/2 cups fresh	1-1/2 cups soy milk
milk in ice cube tray	1 Tbsp honey
8 pitted dates	nutmeg
1 tsp vanilla	

Blend soy milk, dates, honey and vanilla about 2 minutes on high speed until dates are liquified. With blender running on medium speed, add the milk cubes one at a time until shake is thick and creamy. Serve at once with a sprinkle of nutmeg. This is a very delicious shake and tastes as if it contained ice cream. Makes 4 servings.

Variation: Add 2 Tbsp malted milk powder or 1 Tbsp carob powder.

Frosted Soy Egg Nog

Freeze 1-1/2 cups fresh	1-1/2 cups soy milk
milk in ice cube tray	2 Tbsp honey
2 eggs	nutmeg
1 tsp vanilla	

Blend eggs in blender for 30 seconds. Add soy milk, honey and vanilla and blend 10 seconds. With blender running on medium speed, add milk cubes one at a time until drink is thick and creamy. Serve immediately with a sprinkle of nutmeg. Makes 4 servings.

Vegetable Sprout Cocktail

1 cup alfalfa sprouts	1/4 cup lentil sprouts
2 Tbsp parsley	1 green onion, chopped
1/4 cup diced celery	1/4 cup green pepper,
1/2 cup sliced, unpeeled	diced
cucumber	1/4 cup diced carrots
1/8 tsp celery salt	dash Tabasco sauce
1 Tbsp lemon juice	3 cups tomato juice

Pour 1-1/2 cups tomato juice in blender and add Tabasco sauce, lemon juice, celery salt and one half of the vegetables and sprouts. Blend on high speed for about 2 minutes or until vegetables have liquified. Strain through a coarse strainer. Blend remaining tomato juice and vegetables until liquified. Strain through coarse strainer and combine the two portions. Stir well and chill before serving. Makes 6 servings.

Alfa-Mint Cooler

1 cup alfalfa sprouts
1 Tbsp lemon juice
10 fresh mint leaves
1 Tbsp honey

2-1/2 cups unsweetened
pineapple juice
1/2 cup cracked ice

Pour 1-1/2 cups pineapple juice and remaining ingredients into blender and blend on high speed for about one minute. Strain through coarse strainer, add remaining pineapple juice and stir to blend. Place 2 Tbsp cracked ice in each glass and pour juice over it. Makes 4 servings.

Alfalfa Berry Frosty

1 cup alfalfa sprouts
2 Tbsp lemon juice
1 cup fresh raspberries or
    strawberries
4 thin slices lemon

2-1/2 cups unsweetened
pineapple juice
2 Tbsp honey
1/2 cup cracked ice

Blend 1-1/2 cups pineapple juice and remaining ingredients except lemon slices and ice until smooth. Strain through coarse strainer and stir in remaining pineapple juice. Place 2 Tbsp cracked ice in each glass and pour juice over it. Garnish with lemon slice. Makes 4 servings.

Chlorophyll Sprout Special

1 cup alfalfa sprouts
1/4 cup parsley
1-1/2 cups pineapple juice
1 Tbsp lemon juice

2 Tbsp cress sprouts
1/4 cup mint leaves
1 cup cold water

Pour pineapple juice into blender and add alfalfa and cress sprouts and blend for one minute. Pour in water and add remaining ingredients. Blend on high speed for 2 or 3 minutes until smooth. Strain through coarse strainer and serve cold. Makes 4 servings.

CHAPTER X

RECIPES FOR BREADS

General Information on Making Bread with Sprouts

Sprouts can be added to almost any favorite yeast or quick bread recipe by substituting fresh or ground dried sprouts for part of the flour. If fresh sprouts are used, reduce the amount of liquid. Start with a small amount of sprouts in any recipe, and then increase gradually until desired results are obtained. Always use grain sprouts when the shoot is no more than half the length of the grain, or when it is barely showing. Longer shoots indicate that the sprout has a higher percentage of water, and baked products will be soggy. Always dry sprouts well between paper toweling before grinding. As a general rule, breads containing fresh sprouts should be baked 10 percent longer than the original recipe recommends. Any white flour can be used instead of the unbleached.

Wheat Sprout Muffins

1/2 cup ground wheat
    sprouts
1 cup unbleached white
    flour
1/2 tsp salt
1 cup milk
2 beaten eggs

1 cup whole wheat
    flour
4 tsp baking powder
1/3 cup brown sugar
1/3 cup cooking oil
    (soy)

Sift dry ingredients into mixing bowl. Combine milk, eggs and oil and stir sprouts into mixture. Add to dry ingredients and stir only enough to moisten. Fill greased muffin pans 2/3 full of batter and bake in 400° oven for 20 minutes. Makes 12 large muffins.

Variations: Any of the following ingredients may be added to the dry ingredients for delicious muffins. 1/2 cup chopped nuts, 1/2 cup chopped dates or raisins, 4 strips crumbled bacon or 1/4 cup soy sprout nuts, 3/4 cup grated cheese, 1/2 cup drained blueberries or chopped cranberries, replace 3/4 cup whole wheat flour with 3/4 cup wheat germ or cornmeal, replace 1/4 cup milk with orange juice and add 2 Tbsp grated orange rind.

Wheat Sprout Baking Powder Biscuits

1 cup ground wheat sprouts	1 cup unbleached white flour
1 cup whole wheat flour	1/2 tsp salt
4 tsp baking powder	1/2 tsp cream of tartar
2 tsp sugar	1/2 cup shortening
2/3 cup milk (approx.)	

Sift dry ingredients together and cut in shortening. Combine half the milk with the wheat sprouts and add to dry ingredients. Add enough of the remaining milk to make a soft dough. Turn out on lightly floured board and knead lightly three or four times. Pat or roll to 3/4 inch thickness. Cut with floured cutter and bake on greased baking sheet in 400° oven for 15 minutes. Makes 16 biscuits.

Variation: Substitute 1 cup cornmeal for 1 cup whole wheat flour; add 3/4 cup grated cheese to basic recipe, add 2 Tbsp chopped pimiento.

Sprouted Wheat Popovers

3/4 cup ground wheat sprouts	1-3/4 cups unbleached white flour
1 tsp sugar	1/2 tsp salt
1 tsp baking powder	3 beaten eggs
1-3/4 cups milk	2 Tbsp cooking oil

Sift together dry ingredients. Combine milk, eggs, oil and sprouts. Stir to mix and add to dry ingredients. Beat until thoroughly blended. Pour batter into 12 ungreased 5 or 6 ounce heat-resistant glass custard cups, filling them half full. Bake in 425° oven for 15 minutes. Reduce heat to 350° and bake 35 minutes longer. Serve hot with butter. Makes 12 popovers.

Currant Rye Sprout Scones

1/2 cup ground rye sprouts	2 cups unbleached white flour
3 tsp baking powder	

3 Tbsp sugar
1/2 cup evaporated milk
2 beaten eggs
3/4 cup thick strawberry
 or raspberry jam

3/4 tsp salt
1/2 cup shortening
1 cup currants
2 Tbsp soft butter

Rinse and drain currants. Sift together flour, baking powder, salt and sugar. Cut in shortening. Combine beaten eggs, milk, currants and ground sprouts and mix well. Add to flour mixture and stir just enough to moisten. Dough should be soft. Add more milk if necessary. Turn out on lightly floured board and divide in half. Pat each half into a circle 3/8 inch thick. Fit one circle into well-buttered round cake pan, pressing dough 1/4 inch up the side of the pan. Spread with 1 Tbsp soft butter and the jam. Cover with the other circle of dough and spread with 1 Tbsp soft butter. Cut through dough with sharp knife dividing it into 6 wedges. Bake in 400° oven for 25 to 30 minutes. Serve hot. Makes 6 servings.

Corn Sprout Dumplings

1 cup finely ground dried
 corn sprouts
1 tsp salt
2 beaten eggs
1/2 tsp sugar

1 cup unbleached white
 flour
3 tsp baking powder
1/2 cup milk
4 Tbsp salad oil

Sift dry ingredients together into large bowl. Combine milk, eggs and oil and add to dry ingredients all at once. Stir only to moisten, do not beat. Drop heaping teaspoons of batter onto buttered surface of steamer set over boiling water or stew. Cover and steam for 20 minutes without lifting the lid. Serve with hot chicken or beef stew or with thickened fruit sauce for a dessert. Makes 4 servings.

Banana Nut Wheat Bread

1/2 cup ground wheat
 sprouts
3/4 cup brown sugar
1 cup mashed bananas
2 beaten eggs

1-1/2 cups unbleached
 white flour
1/2 cup shortening
1 tsp vanilla
2 tsp baking powder

1/2 tsp salt   1/2 tsp cinnamon
1/2 cup chopped walnuts

Cream sugar and shortening. Stir in bananas, vanilla and eggs. Beat well, add sprouts and beat again. Add sifted dry ingredients and nuts and stir only until well mixed. Bake in 325° oven 1 hour and 10 minutes in well-buttered loaf pan. Makes 1 loaf.

Spicy Apple Bread

1/2 cup ground wheat   3/4 cup dark brown sugar
  sprouts   1 cup grated raw apple
2 eggs   1/2 cup chopped walnuts
1/4 cup buttermilk   2 cups unbleached
1/2 cup shortening   white flour
1/2 tsp salt   1/2 tsp soda
1 tsp cinnamon   1/2 tsp nutmeg
1/4 tsp cloves

Sift together dry ingredients and set aside. Combine shortening, sugar and eggs and beat well. Stir in apple, sprouts and half the dry ingredients. Add the buttermilk and blend. Add remaining flour mixture and stir just to blend. Stir in nuts. Pour into greased loaf pan and bake in 350° oven for 45 minutes. Cool on rack. Let stand overnight before slicing. Makes 1 loaf.

Orange Nut Loaf

1/2 cup ground rye sprouts   2-3/4 cups unbleached
1/2 tsp salt   white flour
1/2 cup brown sugar,   4 tsp baking powder
  packed   1/2 cup walnuts, chopped
1 beaten egg   1 cup milk
1/4 cup orange juice   4 Tbsp cooking oil
2 Tbsp grated orange rind

Sift flour with salt, baking powder and sugar. Add nuts and sprouts and mix to distribute evenly. Combine remaining ingredients and add to dry ingredients. Stir until just mixed, do not beat. Turn into greased loaf pan and bake in 350° oven for 1 hour. Let cool 20 minutes and remove from pan to finish cooling. Let stand overnight before slicing. Makes 1 large or 2 small loaves. Reduce baking time to 50 minutes for small loaves.

Date Nut Bread

1/2 cup ground wheat sprouts	3 tsp baking powder
1-1/2 cups brown sugar	2 cups chopped dates
2 eggs	1-3/4 cups boiling water
3/4 tsp salt	1 tsp soda
2 cups unbleached white flour	2 tsp vanilla
2 cups whole wheat flour	1/4 cup butter
	1 cup chopped walnuts

Sprinkle soda over dates and pour boiling water over them. Let cool to lukewarm. Cream butter and sugar and add beaten eggs and beat well. Stir in sprouts and vanilla. Sift flour, salt and baking powder and add alternately with date mixture. Stir in nuts. Pour into two greased loaf pans and let stand 10 minutes. Bake in 350° oven for 1 hour. Cool on rack for 20 minutes, remove from pans and cool completely before slicing. Makes 2 loaves.

Sprouted Wheat Bread

1 cup wheat sprouts, ground	2 cups whole wheat flour
1 cup wheat sprouts, whole	1 cake yeast (or pkg)
1 tsp sugar	1/4 cup warm water
4 Tbsp oil	4 Tbsp molasses
2-1/2 cups scalded milk (or use warm water and powdered milk)	1 Tbsp salt
	4 cups unbleached white flour (approx.)

Dissolve sugar in 1/4 cup warm water and add yeast. Let stand until yeast bubbles up. Combine hot milk, shortening, molasses and salt in large mixing bowl. When cooled to about 90 degrees, add whole wheat flour and beat well. Add yeast and 2 cups white flour and beat again. Cover and let rise in a warm place about 1 hour or until nearly double. Stir in whole sprouts, ground sprouts and enough white flour to make a soft dough. Mix until dough forms a ball in the bowl. Cover and let stand 15 minutes. Sprinkle 1/2 cup white flour on kneading board and turn out dough. Knead until smooth and elastic, adding more flour as needed to make a medium stiff dough. Place in oiled bowl, cover and let rise until almost double in bulk. Punch down, divide in half, cover and let rest 10 minutes on kneading board. Shape into loaves and put in well-greased bread pans. Let rise until not quite doubled. Bake in preheated 375° oven 45 to 50 minutes. Remove from pans and cool on rack. Makes 2 loaves.

Variation: Substitute rye sprouts for the wheat sprouts and 2 cups rye flour for the whole wheat flour. Add 1 Tbsp caraway seeds if desired.

Sourdough Sprouted Wheat Bread

If possible to secure a start of sourdough, by all means try this delicious sourdough bread.

3 cups starter sponge	1 Tbsp salt
4 Tbsp oil	3/4 cup wheat sprouts, ground
4 Tbsp molasses	
1/2 cup warm water	3/4 cup wheat sprouts, whole
4 cups unbleached white flour	1-1/2 cups whole wheat flour

Beat together starter, warm water, oil and molasses. Stir in whole wheat flour, salt and sprouts. Beat until smooth. Add white flour, 1 cup at a time to make medium stiff dough. Beat with wooden spoon until dough forms ball. Turn out onto floured board and knead about 10 minutes, or until smooth and elastic. Add white flour as needed to make fairly stiff dough. Cover and let rest on board for 10 minutes. Divide in half and form into two loaves. Place in well-greased loaf pans, cover with cloth and let rise in warm place until nearly doubled. This may take longer than it would for yeast bread, but do not bake until it is nearly doubled. The bread will develop the sourdough flavor as it stands. Bake in a 375° oven for 50 minutes. Cool on rack 5 minutes, turn out onto rack and cool before storing. Makes 2 loaves.

Variation: Sourdough Sprouted Rye Bread. Use the above recipe, substituting rye sprouts for the wheat sprouts, and rye flour for the whole wheat flour. Add 1 Tbsp caraway seeds if desired. *Rye Bread Sticks.* Form dough into rolls about 8 inches long and 1/2 inch in diameter. Roll in sesame or caraway seeds, let rise and bake. *Wheat Bread Sticks.* Form wheat dough into bread sticks and roll in cornmeal before baking.

Sprouted Pinto Bean Bread

2 cups pinto bean
  sprouts, cooked 30
  minutes and mashed
1/4 cup warm water
1 tsp sugar
2 Tbsp brown sugar
3 Tbsp oil

4 cups unbleached white
  flour (approx.)
2 pkgs yeast
3/4 cup scalded milk
2 tsp salt
2 cups whole wheat flour

Soften yeast in warm water and 1 tsp sugar. Combine brown sugar, salt, oil, hot milk, beans and whole wheat flour. Stir to mix and add softened yeast. Beat 2 minutes. Add 2 cups white flour and beat 2 minutes longer. Stir in enough of the remaining flour to make a medium soft dough. Turn out onto floured board and knead until smooth and elastic. Place in oiled bowl and let rise in warm place about 1 hour until doubled. Punch down, turn over in bowl and let rise again about 30 minutes. Divide dough in half and shape into loaves. Place in well-greased bread pans, cover and let rise until almost doubled. Do not let it get too light. Bake in pre-heated 375° oven for 45 minutes. Remove from oven and cool 5 minutes. Turn out of pans and cool on racks. Makes 2 loaves.

Sprouted Pinto Bean French Bread

1-1/2 cups pinto bean
  sprouts, cooked 30
  minutes and mashed
1/4 cup warm water
2 Tbsp sugar
1 cup evaporated milk

3 Tbsp oil
6 cups unbleached white
  flour (approx.)
2 pkgs yeast
3/4 cup hot bean juice
1-1/2 tsp salt

Soften yeast in 1/4 cup warm water and 1 tsp sugar. Combine bean juice, milk, salt, oil, remaining sugar and mashed bean sprouts. Add 3 cups flour and the softened yeast and beat 2 minutes. Add enough of the remaining flour to make a medium stiff dough. Turn out on floured board and knead until smooth and elastic. Place in oiled bowl and let rise until double. Punch down and let rise 30 minutes longer. Punch down and turn out onto lightly floured board. Divide into 4 portions and form each one into a roll about 2 inches in diameter. Lightly grease two cookie sheets and place two rolls on each sheet. Let rise until not quite doubled. Brush rolls with cold water and make diagonal slashes in top with a sharp knife. Bake in a 375° oven for 40 minutes. Place shallow pan of hot water in bottom of oven during baking time. Makes 4 rolls of bread.

Orange-Fig Round Bread

1 cup wheat sprouts, ground	2 Tbsp softened butter
1/4 cup lukewarm water	1 pkg yeast
4 Tbsp oil	3 Tbsp brown sugar
2 cups scalded milk	1 Tbsp salt
3 cups unbleached white flour (approx.)	2 cups whole wheat flour
	1 cup chopped black figs
3 Tbsp grated orange rind	1/4 cup brown sugar

Soften yeast in warm water and 1 tsp sugar. Combine scalded milk, oil, 3 Tbsp brown sugar and salt in large mixing bowl. Cool to 90 degrees and add whole wheat flour, yeast and sprouts. Beat two minutes. Stir in enough white flour to make a soft dough and mix until dough forms a ball in bowl. Cover and let stand 10 minutes. Turn out on floured board and knead until smooth and elastic, adding flour as needed. Place in oiled bowl and let rise in warm place until doubled. Punch down and let rest on board 10 minutes. Roll out on floured board to about 12 x 8 inch rectangle. Spread with softened butter and sprinkle the finely chopped figs over the dough. Mix the brown sugar and orange rind and sprinkle over the figs. Take floured rolling pin and roll lightly to press into dough. Roll up, beginning on the 14-inch side. Seal edges and cut roll in half. Drop each half in a well-greased 48 ounce pineapple juice can. Let rise until almost double. Bake in 375° oven for 40 minutes. Let stand 5 minutes, remove from can and cool on rack. Slice in rounds to serve. Makes 2 loaves.

Rolled Cinnamon Rye Loaf

1 cup ground rye sprouts
1/4 cup warm water
1/4 cup oil
1 tsp salt
5 cups unbleached white
   flour (approx.)
1 Tbsp melted butter

1 pkg yeast
1 cup scalded milk
1/2 cup sugar
2 beaten eggs
1 tsp cinnamon
1/4 cup sugar

Soften yeast in warm water and 1 tsp sugar. Combine scalded milk, oil, and 1/2 cup sugar in large mixing bowl. Cool to 90 degrees and add 2 cups flour, eggs, sprouts and yeast. Beat two minutes until smooth. Stir in enough of the remaining flour to make a soft dough and mix until dough forms a ball in bowl. Cover and let stand 15 minutes. Turn out on floured board and knead until smooth and elastic, adding flour as needed. Put in oiled bowl and let rise in warm place until double in bulk. Punch down and let rest on board 10 minutes. Roll out on floured board to about 12 x 8 inch rectangle. Spread with melted butter and sprinkle with cinnamon and 1/4 cup sugar, which have been mixed together. Roll up beginning on the 14 inch side. Seal edges and cut roll in half. Put each half in greased bread pan. Brush with melted butter and sprinkle cinnamon and sugar on top. Let rise until almost doubled. Bake in a 375° oven for 40 minutes. Makes 2 loaves.

Variation: May also be baked in pineapple juice cans. *Cinnamon Rolls:* Sprinkle rolled out dough with raisins in addition to the cinnamon and sugar. Cut into 1-inch pieces and bake on cookie sheets for approximately 20 minutes after rising.

Sesame Oat Sprout Bread

1-1/2 cups oat sprouts,
   ground
1/4 cup molasses
1/4 cup warm water
4 Tbsp oil
2-1/2 cups scalded milk
6 cups unbleached white
   flour (approx.)

1/4 cup sesame seeds,
   ground
1 tsp sugar
1 pkg yeast
1 Tbsp salt
1 Tbsp sesame seeds,
   whole

Soften yeast in warm water and 1 tsp sugar. Combine hot milk, oil, salt and molasses in large bowl. Cool to about 90 degrees and add yeast and 3 cups flour and beat 3 minutes. Cover and let rise until about doubled. Stir in oat sprouts and ground sesame seeds and beat well. Add enough of the remaining flour to make a soft dough. Turn out on well-floured board and knead until smooth and elastic, adding more flour as needed to make a medium stiff dough. Place in oiled bowl, cover and let rise until doubled. Punch down, divide in half and let rest 10 minutes on board. Shape into 2 loaves and place in well-greased bread pans. Brush tops with oil and sprinkle with whole sesame seeds. Let rise until almost doubled. Bake in 375° oven for 45 minutes. Makes 2 loaves.

Variation: Add 1 cup chopped raisins with the sprouts.

Corn Sprout Batter Bread

1-1/2 cups dried corn sprouts, ground	1-1/2 tsp salt
1/2 cup warm water	2 pkgs yeast
1/4 cup butter or oil	1 tsp sugar
4 cups unbleached white flour	1/3 cup molasses
	2 cups scalded milk

Soften yeast in warm water and sugar. Pour hot milk over ground corn sprouts, butter, molasses and salt. Stir well and let cool to lukewarm. Beat in 2 cups flour and softened yeast and beat 2 minutes. Add remaining flour and beat well. Spoon into two well-greased bread pans or four or five 1-pound fruit cocktail cans. Let rise in warm place until nearly doubled. Bake in a 375° oven for about 40 minutes for pans and 25 or 30 minutes for cans. Makes 2 loaves or 4 or 5 cans.

Sprouted Wheat Herb Bread

1 cup ground wheat sprouts	3/4 cup milk
1 pkg onion soup mix (1-3/8 oz.)	1/4 cup brown sugar
1/2 cup butter	2 pkgs yeast
1/2 cup warm water	1 beaten egg
1 tsp sage	1 tsp dried parsley
1 tsp salt	3-1/2 cup unbleached white flour (approx.)

Scald milk and stir in onion mix, butter and sugar. Sprinkle yeast over warm water and stir to dissolve. Add to the warm milk mixture along with the egg, seasonings and half the flour. Beat 3 minutes. Add remaining flour and beat well. Cover and chill at least 2 hours. Cut dough in half, flatten and press evenly into 2 well-buttered bread pans or casseroles (1½ qts). Brush with melted butter, cover and let rise until doubled. Bake in a 375° oven for 40 minutes. Remove from pans and cool on rack. Brush tops with melted butter while warm. Makes 2 loaves.

Onion Wheat Buns

1 cup ground wheat sprouts
3 Tbsp butter
3 Tbsp oil
2 pkg yeast
1-3/4 cups hot water
3 cups unbleached white
    flour (approx.)

3/4 cup chopped onion
3 Tbsp sugar
2 tsp salt
1/4 cup warm water
2 cups whole wheat flour
Onion salt and Paprika

Saute onions in butter until golden. Soften yeast in 1/4 cup warm water and 1 tsp sugar. Blend 1 cup whole wheat flour, 1 cup white flour, sugar, salt and oil. Add hot water and beat 2 minutes. Add cooked onions, yeast and wheat sprouts. Beat 2 minutes. Add balance of the whole wheat flour and 1 cup white flour or enough to make a soft dough. Turn out on floured board and knead until smooth and elastic. Place in oiled bowl and let rise in warm place until doubled. Punch down and divide into 24 pieces. Roll each one into a ball and place on buttered baking sheet. Flatten each into a four-inch circle. Turn so buttered side is up. Sprinkle lightly with onion salt and paprika. Let rise until doubled. Bake in 375° oven for 20 to 25 minutes. Makes 24 buns.

Molasses Wheat Refrigerator Rolls

1 cup wheat sprouts, ground
1/2 cup warm water
2/3 cup molasses
2 tsp salt
2 cups whole wheat flour
1 tsp sugar

2 pkgs yeast
1-1/2 cups scalded milk
1/3 cup shortening
2 beaten eggs
3-1/2 cups unbleached
    white flour (approx.)

Dissolve yeast in warm water and sugar. Scald milk and add salt, oil and molasses and cool to lukewarm. Add eggs, yeast and whole wheat flour and beat well. Add half of the white flour and beat again. Add remaining flour and beat well. Cover tightly and store in refrigerator overnight before making into rolls. Form into rolls in desired shape and size and let rise until doubled. Chilled dough will take longer to get light, so allow more time for rising. Bake in a 375° oven 12 to 15 minutes. Makes 36 small rolls.

Golden Corn Sprout Rolls

2/3 cups dried corn sprouts, finely ground
1-1/2 tsp salt
1/4 cup warm water
2 beaten eggs
4 cups unbleached white flour (approx.)
1/2 cup honey or sugar
1/2 cup oil or butter
1/2 cup finely mashed carrots, cooked
1-1/2 cups scalded milk
1 pkg yeast

Soften yeast in warm water and 1 tsp sugar. Scald milk, add corn sprouts and cook 5 minutes. Remove from heat and add honey, shortening and carrots. Cool to lukewarm and add yeast, eggs and 2 cups flour. Beat 2 minutes. Add remaining flour to make a soft dough. Turn out on floured board and knead until smooth, adding more flour to keep from sticking. Place in oiled bowl, cover and let rise in warm place until doubled. Punch down and shape into rolls. Let rise until doubled and bake in 375° oven 12 to 15 minutes. Makes 24 medium rolls.

Raised Rye Sprout Muffins

3/4 cup rye sprouts
2 cups warm water
2 Tbsp sugar
3 beaten eggs
1/2 cup currants
1/2 cup sugar
1 tsp cinnamon
1 pkg yeast
1/2 cup powdered milk
2 tsp salt
3/4 cup oil
5 cups unbleached white flour (approx.)

Dissolve yeast in 1 cup warm water and 1 tsp sugar. Combine eggs, powdered milk, sugar, salt, oil, yeast mixture and 3 cups flour. Beat well. Add currants, rye sprouts and enough addional flour to make a medium stiff dough. Beat again, cover and let rise until doubled. Drop batter into greased muffin pans, filling 2/3 full. Sprinkle with cinnamon and sugar. Let rise until doubled. Bake in 375° oven for 15 to 20 minutes. Makes 24 large muffins.

Crunchy Cheese Rounds

1 cup dried ground soy sprouts	1 cup shredded sharp cheddar cheese
1 cup unbleached white flour	1/2 cup soft butter or
dash cayenne pepper	margarine

Mix butter and cheese in bowl until thoroughly combined. Add flour, cayenne pepper and soy sprouts. Mix well. Drop by rounded teaspoons onto ungreased baking sheets. Flatten to 1/4 inch thickness with bottom of glass which has been greased and dipped in flour. Bake in 325° oven about 20 minutes or until lightly browned. Serve warm or cold. Makes 24 rounds.

Sprouted Rye Crisp

2 cups rye sprouts, ground fine	1 tsp salt

Spread ground sprouts on lightly greased cookie sheet to 1/8 inch thick. Sprinkle evenly with salt and bake in very slow oven—120° for 30 minutes. Remove pan from oven and mark into squares with knife. Return to oven and continue baking at 120° about 20 minutes longer or until dry. Makes 6 doz. 1-1/2 inch squares.
Variation: Sprinkle with season salt, garlic salt, sesame or caraway seed.

Sprouted Wheat Crisp

Follow above recipe, using 2 cups of wheat sprouts ground fine. Season with salt, season salt, garlic salt, barbeque salt, etc.

Sprouted Wheat Thins

1 cup whole wheat flour	1 cup dried wheat sprouts
2 cups water	1 tsp salt

Grind dried wheat sprouts very fine in grinder or in blender until almost as fine as whole wheat flour. Combine with flour and salt and add water. Stir until smooth. Pour about 1/2 cup of the thin batter on a well-greased cookie sheet and tilt to spread evenly. Sprinkle with garlic salt, onion salt, season salt or sesame seeds if desired. Bake in 375° oven for about 15 minutes or until lightly browned. When cool break into pieces. Makes about 6 doz. 1-1/2 inch squares.

Variation: Use dried sprouted rye instead of the sprouted wheat with one cup of unbleached white flour or part rye flour. Fill a squirt bottle with the thin batter and form into various shapes on greased cookie sheet.

Sprouted Wheat Wafers

1 cup whole wheat flour	1 cup dried wheat sprouts
1/2 tsp salt	1 tsp baking powder
1/2 cup cream or evaporated milk (approx.)	2 Tbsp oil

Grind wheat sprouts very fine in food grinder or in blender. Combine sprouts, flour, oil, salt and baking powder together and mix well. Stir in enough cream to make a medium soft dough. Knead lightly and roll out on lightly floured board 1/8 inch or less. With sharp knife cut into squares or any desired shape. Bake on lightly greased baking sheet 375° about 8 minutes or until lightly browned. Makes about 5 dozen 1-1/2 inch squares.

Variation: Substitute rye sprouts for wheat sprouts and use white and part rye flour. Sprinkle with any desired seasoning or seeds. Use 1 cup dried corn sprouts and 1 cup white flour and sprinkle with dry onion soup mix before baking.

Sprouted Graham Crackers

1-1/2 cups ground wheat sprouts, dried	1-1/2 cups whole wheat flour
2 Tbsp honey	3 Tbsp water (approx.)
3 Tbsp oil	1/4 tsp salt
1/2 tsp baking powder	

Combine oil, honey and water and mix to blend thoroughly. Stir ground sprouts, flour, baking powder and salt together and add to the liquid ingredients. Mix with fork until dough leaves sides of the bowl. Turn out onto waxed paper lightly sprinkled with flour and form into a roll 1-1/2 inches in diameter. Roll in waxed paper and chill. Slice 1/8 inch thick, place on greased baking sheet and prick with fork. Bake in 375° oven for 8 to 10 minutes. Makes 24 crackers.

CHAPTER XI

RECIPES FOR BREAKFASTS

Baked Wheat Sprout Pancakes

1 cup ground wheat sprouts	1 cup unbleached white
1 tsp salt	flour
4 tsp baking powder	1 cup whole wheat flour
4 Tbsp brown sugar	2 cups milk
4 Tbsp oil	2 egg yolks
2 beaten egg whites	

Sift dry ingredients into a large bowl. Combine milk, egg yolks, oil and sprouts. Add to dry ingredients all at once and stir only to moisten. Gently fold in the stiffly beaten egg whites. Pour batter into well-buttered jelly-roll pan, 15 x 10 x 1 inch. Bake in 425° oven 15 to 20 minutes until the top is lightly browned. Cut into squares and serve with butter and syrup or honey. Serves 4 or 5. This batter may also be cooked on a hot griddle.

Crisp Potato-Wheat Pancakes

1 cup ground wheat sprouts	2 cups grated potato
2 Tbsp grated onion	2 beaten eggs
3 Tbsp flour	1/2 tsp salt
1/4 tsp baking powder	1/8 tsp pepper
2 Tbsp butter	2 Tbsp oil

Grate potato immediately before using to prevent dis-coloring. Drain grated potato and combine with wheat sprouts, onion and beaten egg. Mix well. Combine flour, salt, pepper and baking powder and stir into potato mixture. Heat oil and butter in heavy skillet and drop heaping tablespoons of the mixture into the hot shortening and fry about 5 minutes on each side or until crisp and golden brown. Serve hot with apple sauce and bacon or sausage for a hearty breakfast. Serves 4.

Rye Sprout Pancakes

1/2 cup ground rye sprouts
1/2 cup unbleached white
    flour
2 tsp baking powder
2 Tbsp brown sugar or
    light molasses
3 Tbsp oil

1/2 cup whole wheat flour
1/4 cup powdered milk
    (non instant)
1/2 tsp salt
1 cup milk
3 egg yolks
3 beaten egg whites

Sift flour, salt, baking powder and powdered milk together into mixing bowl and stir in the sprouts. In small bowl combine egg yolks, sugar, oil and milk and mix well. Make a well in in the center of dry mixture and pour in liquid mixture. Mix only until moistened. Fold in beaten egg whites. Cook on lightly greased hot griddle. Serve hot with butter and maple syrup, honey or jam. Makes 4 servings.
    Variations: Substitute wheat or rice sprouts.

Sprout Waffles

1/2 cup ground wheat or
    rye sprouts
3 tsp baking powder
1 Tbsp sugar
4 Tbsp oil
1 cup milk

1 cup unbleached white
    flour
1/2 tsp salt
2 egg yolks
2 egg whites

Sift dry ingredients together twice. Combine egg yolks, sprouts, oil and milk and add to dry ingredients. Beat to blend. Fold in stiffly beaten egg whites. Bake in hot waffle iron. Makes 3 or 4 servings.

Mung Sprout Omelet

1 cup mung bean sprouts
4 egg yolks
1/2 tsp salt
1/2 cup grated cheddar
    cheese

2 Tbsp butter
4 beaten egg whites
1/8 tsp ground pepper
4 Tbsp cream or evaporated
    milk

Chop sprouts and saute in butter in heavy skillet for 3 minutes. Remove sprouts and keep warm. Mix egg yolks, cream, salt and pepper. Fold in beaten egg whites and pour into heavy skillet. Cover and cook over low heat without stirring until set. Place under broiler for about 1 minute to dry top. Sprinkle sprouts and cheese over top, fold over and serve at once. Makes 4 servings.

Scrambled Eggs with Lentils

1/2 cup lentil sprouts	6 eggs
4 Tbsp cream or evaporated milk	1/2 tsp salt
	2 Tbsp butter
1/8 tsp pepper	

Beat eggs lightly and add cream, salt, pepper and lentil sprouts. Heat butter in heavy skillet and pour in the eggs. Cook over low heat stirring frequently until set. Makes 4 servings.

Baked Eggs

1/4 cup dried wheat sprouts, finely ground	4 eggs
4 tsp butter	4 Tbsp cream
	salt, pepper, dillweed

Place 1 tsp butter in 4 ramekins or custard cups. Pour 1 Tbsp cream in each cup and sprinkle with 2 tsp wheat sprouts. Break one egg in each cup and sprinkle with salt, pepper and dillweed. Bake in 350° oven 15 or 20 minutes. Serve hot. Makes 4 servings.

Hot Sprout Cereal

2 cups sprouted wheat or rye	1 cup water
1/4 tsp salt	

Combine sprouts and water in saucepan and bring to boil. Turn to simmer, cover and cook 1/2 hour. Add the salt the last 5 minutes of cooking. Serve hot with sliced bananas and half and half. Makes 6 servings.

Variations: Serve with fresh fruit or berries in season. Stir in 1/2 cup raisins, dates or other dried fruit the last ten minutes of cooking time. Left-over cereal may be reheated as cereal or used whole or ground in other recipes calling for cooked wheat or rye sprouts.

Hot Rye Sprout Cereal

1/2 cup cream of rye cereal	1/2 cup rye sprouts
2 cups boiling water	1/4 tsp salt

Pour water into sauce pan and bring to a boil. Slowly stir in the cream of rye cereal and add the rye sprouts. Cover and cook over low heat for 30 minutes, stirring occasionally. Stir in the salt the last 5 minutes of cooking. Makes 4 or 5 servings. Serve hot with cream or milk.

Variations: Stir in 1/2 cup raisins the last 5 minutes of cooking. Serve with sliced bananas, berries or fruits in season.

Rice Sprout Cereal

2 cups rice sprouts	1 cup water
1/2 cup raisins	1/4 tsp salt

Cook rice sprouts in water for 25 minutes over low heat. Stir in the raisins and salt and cook 5 minutes longer. Serve hot with top milk or cream. Makes 4 or 5 servings.

Sprouted Wheat Flakes

2 cups sprouted wheat	1 tsp salt
2 Tbsp brown sugar	1/2 cup water

Cook wheat 30 minutes in water. Remove lid and cook 5 minutes to let wheat dry out and water boil away. Cool to warm and stir in salt and sugar. Cool completely and grind on fine knife. Leave wheat in ribbons as it comes out of grinder. Bake on lightly greased cookie sheet in a 300° oven for about 30 minutes or until dry. Cool and break into flakes. Serve with milk or cream as a dry cereal. Fruit may be added if desired. Makes 4 to 6 servings.

Malted Wheat Nuts

2 cups sprouted wheat	1/2 cup water
1 tsp salt	2 Tbsp brown sugar
4 Tbsp powdered milk (not instant)	1 Tbsp Malted milk powder

Cook wheat in water for 30 minutes. Cool and grind on fine knife of food grinder. Combine remaining ingredients and mix with ground wheat. Spread 1/4 inch thick on cookie sheet, which has been lightly greased. Bake in 140° oven for about 40 minutes or until dry. Cool, break into pieces and grind on medium knife. Serve as dry cereal with milk or cream. Makes 6 servings.

CHAPTER XII

RECIPES FOR BABY FOODS

Instead of purchasing canned or packaged baby food, sprouts may be used for preparing a variety of nutritious dishes. They taste delicious, contain no preservatives and cost but a fraction of of the cost of prepared foods. The dried sprout powder or granules can be kept on hand to make feedings as needed, or several servings can be prepared and frozen in small portions for later use. Many sprout and meat or fruit combinations can be used, depending what is on hand or what has been cooked for the family.

Instant Sprout Cereal

1 cup wheat sprouts, dried	1 cup rice sprouts, dried
1 cup oat sprouts, dried	1 cup soybean sprouts, dried

Grind the dried sprouts in the blender until they are very fine. Store in air tight jar and use as needed. For serving, stir milk or formula into desired amount of sprout cereal. A raw or lightly cooked egg yolk can also be added if desired. Makes 2 cups of cereal powder.

Any combination of dried sprouts can be used to make the instant cereal. The powder can also be stirred into mashed or pureed vegetables for more nutrition.

Cooked Sprout Breakfast

1/2 cup millet sprouts	1/2 cup wheat sprouts

Cook sprouts in 1 cup water for 45 minutes or until very tender. Force through food mill or puree in blender for small baby. A raw egg yolk may be stirred into the hot cereal and then cooled to feed baby. Stir egg yolk in just before feeding. Store cereal in refrigerator in covered container until ready for use. Makes 4 to 6 servings.

Liver and Sprouts

1/2 cup soy sprouts   1/2 cup lentil sprouts
4 Tbsp cooked chopped liver   1/2 cup broth or water

Steam sprouts in broth 30 minutes or until tender. Add chopped liver and cook 10 minutes longer. Put through food mill or puree in blender for small baby. For older baby mash or chop sprouts. Makes 4 to 6 servings. Store in refrigerator in covered container.

Chicken with Sprouts

1/2 cup rice sprouts   1/2 cup mung bean sprouts
1/2 cup broth or water   4 Tbsp finely chopped
                             chicken, cooked

Cook rice sprouts in broth 30 minutes or until tender. Add mung bean sprouts after 20 minutes of cooking. Add chicken for last 5 minutes of cooking. Force through food mill or puree in blender for small baby and mash or chop sprouts for older baby. Makes 4 to 6 servings. Store in refrigerator in covered container.

Beef with Sprouts

1/2 cup wheat sprouts   1/2 cup lentil sprouts
1/2 cup broth or water   4 Tbsp finely chopped
                             beef, cooked

Cook wheat sprouts in broth for 50 minutes. Add more water or broth if necessary. Add lentil sprouts and beef and cook 10 minutes longer. Force through food mill or puree in blender for small baby. Grind or chop fine for older baby. Makes 4 to 6 servings. Store in refrigerator in covered container.

Veal with Sprouts

1/2 cup rye sprouts   1/4 cup lentil sprouts
1/2 cup water or broth   4 Tbsp finely chopped veal

Cook rye sprouts in broth for 40 minutes. Add lentil sprouts and veal and cook 10 minutes longer. Force through food mill or puree in blender. Grind or chop very fine for older baby.

Lamb with Sprouts

1/2 cup barley sprouts   1/4 cup lentil sprouts
1/2 cup broth or water   4 Tbsp finely chopped
                                        lamb

Cook barley sprouts 40 minutes in broth. Add lentil sprouts and lamb and cook 10 minutes longer. Force through food mill or puree in blender. Chop or grind for older baby. Makes 3 or 4 servings. Store in refrigerator in covered container.

Fruit Sauce and Sprouts

1/4 cup pureed or mashed fruit—apple sauce, peaches, pears, prunes, apricots or bananas. Stir 2 Tbsp instant sprout cereal into the fruit sauce just before serving.

CHAPTER XIII

RECIPES FOR ENTREES

Wheat 'N' Meat Loaf

1-1/2 cups sprouted wheat (1/8 inch sprout)	1/2 cup milk
	1/4 cup chopped onion
3/4 tsp sage	1 beaten egg
1/4 cup catsup	1/8 tsp pepper
1 tsp salt	1 lb lean ground beef
2 Tbsp Worcestershire sauce	

Cook wheat 30 minutes in 1/2 cup water. Cool slightly and stir in milk and beaten egg. Add onion, catsup, ground beef and seasonings. Mix well and pack into greased loaf pan and bake in 325° oven for 1 hour. Remove from oven and let stand 10 minutes. Remove from pan and serve hot plain or with tomato or cheese sauce. Serves 6.

Rice Sprout Bundles

1-1/2 cups rice sprouts	1/4 cup water
2 lbs lean ground beef	1/2 cup minced onions
1 tsp salt	1/4 tsp oregano
1/8 tsp ground pepper	1 beaten egg
2 cups spaghetti sauce with mushrooms	1/4 cup minced green pepper
1/4 cup minced celery	

Cook rice on low heat in water for 20 minutes. Drain and cool. Mix meat, onions, salt, pepper, oregano and egg together. Add 1/4 cup spaghetti sauce and mix well. Press mixture into a 16 x 6 rectangle on waxed paper. Cut into eight 2 x 6 inch pieces. Mix rice sprouts, green pepper, celery and 1/4 cup spaghetti sauce. Divide equally and place in center of meat. Fold meat over rice and form into small loaves completely covering rice. Place in buttered shallow baking pan and spoon remaining spaghetti sauce over them. Bake in 300° oven for 30 minutes. Makes 8 servings.

Curried Beef and Rice Sprouts

3/4 cup lean ground beef	2 Tbsp cress sprouts
1 cup chopped onions	2 cups rice sprouts
1 cup chicken or beef broth	1 Tbsp butter
1/4 cup sliced mushrooms,	1/2 tsp salt
canned	1 tsp curry powder
2 Tbsp Worcestershire sauce	1/2 cup sour cream

Saute onions in butter until transparent. Remove from pan and cook meat until it has lost its color. Add rice and continue cooking and stirring until meat has browned. Add cooked onions and remaining ingredients, except cream and cress sprouts. Bring to a boil, stirring constantly. Reduce heat and simmer 30 minutes. Serve hot topped with a spoonful of sour cream sprinkled with chopped cress sprouts. Makes 4 servings.

Sweet 'N' Sour Beef with Mung Sprouts

2 cups rice sprouts	3 Tbsp cold water
3/4 lb. top round steak,	1/2 cup water
3/4 inch thick	1 cup mung bean sprouts
4 Tbsp oil	1 tsp seasoned meat
1 cup onion, thinly cut	tenderizer
in wedges	1/2 cup water chestnuts,
1/2 cup green pepper, diced	sliced
coarsely	1 cup pineapple tidbits
1/2 cup pineapple juice	1 Tbsp ketchup
2 Tbsp wine vinegar	1 Tbsp soy sauce
1 tsp brown sugar	1 Tbsp cornstarch

Cook rice sprouts in 1/2 cup water for 30 minutes and meanwhile prepare meat. Moisten one side of meat with water and sprinkle with tenderizer. Pierce meat deeply with fork at 1/2 inch intervals. Let stand 5 minutes, turn and repeat on other side. Cut meat across grain into very thin slices. Heat oil in large skillet and brown beef on high heat, stirring constantly. Remove meat and all but 2 Tbsp of drippings from pan. Add onions, water chestnuts and green pepper and saute for 3 minutes. Add pineapple, pineapple juice, ketchup, vinegar, soy sauce, sugar and bean sprouts and heat to boiling. Mix cornstarch with cold water and add to mixture in skillet. Stir until sauce thickens. Add meat and drippings and heat to boiling. Serve over the hot cooked rice sprouts. Makes 4 servings.

Barbequed Chicken Legs

1 cup soy sprouts, roasted
   and ground very fine
8 chicken drumsticks
salt and pepper to taste

1 beaten egg
1/4 cup garlic flavored
   barbecue sauce

Combine egg and barbecue sauce. Dip chicken legs in mixture and sprinkle with salt and pepper if desired. Roll in ground soy sprouts. Place on rack of broiler pan and bake in 350° oven for 1 hour, or until tender. Makes 4 servings.

Sprouted Green Rice Casserole

2 cups rice sprouts
2 Tbsp melted butter
1/2 cup hot milk
1 Tbsp minced chives
2 Tbsp minced parsley
1/8 tsp ground pepper

1/2 cup grated nippy cheese
1 beaten egg
1 Tbsp minced green onion
2 Tbsp minced green pepper
1/2 tsp salt
Paprika

Combine all ingredients except paprika. Pour into buttered casserole about 8 x 8 inches. Do not have rice more than 1-1/2 inches deep. Bake in 325° oven 45 to 50 minutes. Delicious served with chicken or ham. Makes 6 servings.

Cornmeal Sprout Souffle

1 cup mung bean sprouts,
   chopped
2 Tbsp butter
1/4 cup cornmeal
1/8 tsp pepper

1 cup milk
3/4 cup sharp cheddar
   cheese
3/4 tsp salt
4 eggs, separated

Combine milk, butter, cornmeal, salt and pepper in heavy saucepan. Cook and stir over low heat until thick and smooth. Add grated cheese and continue stirring until melted. Stir in chopped sprouts. Beat egg yolks with rotary beater until thick.

Fold through cheese mixture. Beat egg whites stiff, but not dry and fold gently into mixture. Pour into buttered 1-1/2 quart casserole. Set in shallow pan of boiling water and bake in 350° oven for 50 to 60 minutes until knife comes out clean. Serve at once. Makes 4 servings.

Soy Cheese Pudding

1 cup soy sprouts, steamed
   20 minutes
1-1/2 cups milk
1/2 tsp salt
3 slices buttered whole
   wheat bread, cubed

twist or two of black pepper
3 eggs
1/2 tsp dry mustard
1 cup sharp cheese, cubed
dash cayenne pepper

Arrange half of the cubed bread in a buttered casserole. Top with half the cubed cheese and half the soy sprouts. Repeat a second layer with the remaining bread, cheese and sprouts. Beat eggs, add milk and seasonings. Pour over bread, sprinkle with paprika and bake in a 350° oven 45 minutes. Makes 4 servings.

Soy Macaroni and Cheese

1 cup soy sprouts,
   steamed 10 minutes
1/2 lb. sharp cheddar
   cheese, grated
1 tall can evaporated milk
1 tsp dry mustard
4 Tbsp butter

1/8 tsp ground pepper
1-1/2 cups macaroni
6 cups water
2 beaten eggs
2 tsp grated onion
3/4 tsp salt
paprika

Cook macaroni in boiling water and 3/4 tsp salt until tender. Drain and place in buttered 1-1/2 quart casserole with soy sprouts. Add the butter and stir to melt. Stir in 3/4 of the cheese. Combine milk, eggs, onion, mustard and pepper and pour over the macaroni. Top with the remaining cheese and sprinkle generously with paprika. Bake in a 350° oven about 25 minutes. Do not overbake or it will be too dry. Makes 4 servings.

Wheat Sprout Fritters

1 cup wheat sprouts,
  ground
1 cup sharp cheese,
  grated
1/2 tsp salt
2 Tbsp soy sauce
1 Tbsp butter

1/4 cup minced onion
1/2 cup beef stock
1/8 tsp pepper
1 cup whole wheat bread
  crumbs
2 Tbsp oil

Combine all ingredients, mix well and form into patties. Heat butter and oil in heavy skillet and fry until crisp and brown. Makes 4 servings.

Lentil-Potato Crisp

4 medium potatoes
1/2 can cream of chicken
  soup
1/4 cup milk
1/2 cup grated cheddar
  cheese
1/8 tsp pepper
1/2 cup fine dry bread
  crumbs

2 cups lentil sprouts
1/2 cup sour cream
1/4 cup chopped green
  onions
1/4 tsp salt
2 Tbsp melted butter
paprika

Boil potatoes until not quite done. Peel and cool. Grate on a coarse grater and mix with all ingredients except bread crumbs, butter and paprika. Pour into a well-buttered baking dish about 9 x 9 inches. Combine butter with bread crumbs and sprinkle over top. Sprinkle with paprika. Bake in 375° oven for 30 minutes. Serves 4.

Oriental Fried Rice

2 cups cold cooked rice
  sprouts
1 cup shredded cooked
  meat (chicken, pork,
  shrimp or ham)
1/4 cup finely chopped
  green onion

1/2 cup sliced mushrooms,
  fresh or canned
1/2 tsp salt
4 Tbsp butter or oil
2 Tbsp soy sauce
1/8 tsp pepper

Heat butter in heavy skillet. Saute onion until golden brown. Add meat and mushrooms and stir-fry 1 minute. Add rice and soy sauce and cook, stirring, over medium heat for 10 minutes. Makes 4 to 6 servings.

Note: Rice sprouts should be cold and slightly dry before frying.

Spanish Rice Sprouts

2 cups rice sprouts	1 cup cooked tomatoes
1/2 lb. ground beef	8 oz. tomato sauce
1 Tbsp oil	1/2 cup chopped onion
1 clove garlic, chopped	1/2 cup chopped green
1/4 tsp oregano	pepper
1/2 tsp salt	1/4 tsp chili powder
1 Tbsp minced parsley	1/8 tsp pepper

Brown the meat in the oil, stirring to break into small pieces. Drain off any fat, add onion and garlic and cook 1 minute. Add the remaining ingredients and mix well. Bring to a boil, cover and turn to very low heat. Cook for 30 minutes, stirring occasionally. Serve hot. Makes 4 servings.

Cooked Ground Soy Sprouts

2 cups soy sprouts	1/2 cup water
1/2 tsp salt	

Grind soy sprouts, using medium knife of food grinder. Cook over very low heat, stirring frequently, for 30 minutes. Add salt and cook 5 minutes longer. Add a small amount of water, if necessary, to keep the sprouts from sticking. Cool and store in covered container in refrigerator. Use these ground sprouts in any recipe calling for cooked ground soy sprouts. Makes 2 cups.

Cooking Bean Sprouts

Always cook bean sprouts of any kind in plain water. Do not add salt or any other seasoning until they are tender. Salt will slow the cooking process and the flavor will not be as good.

Soy Sprout Loaf

2 cups ground cooked
  soy sprouts
1 beaten egg
1/2 cup grated carrot
1/8 tsp pepper
1/4 tsp oregano leaves

1/4 cup tomato sauce
1/2 cup chopped onion
1/2 cup tomato sauce
1/2 tsp salt
1/4 tsp chili powder
1/2 cup wheat germ

Combine all ingredients except 1/4 cup tomato sauce and mix to blend. Pack into oiled loaf pan and spread 1/4 cup tomato sauce on top. Bake in 350° oven 40 minutes. Makes 4 servings.

Lentil-Soy Sprout Loaf

1 cup ground cooked soy
  sprouts
1/2 cup minced onion
1/4 cup minced celery
1 cup whole wheat bread
  crumbs
1/8 tsp nutmeg

1/2 tsp salt
1-1/2 cups lentil sprouts,
  cook 10 minutes
2 beaten eggs
1/4 cup tomato sauce
1 clove garlic, minced
1/8 tsp pepper

Mix all ingredients together and pack into buttered loaf pan. Bake in 350° oven for 35 minutes. Let stand 10 minutes and invert on platter to serve. Serve plain or with tomato sauce or ketchup. Makes 4 servings.

Soy Sprout Sausage

3 cups cooked soy
  sprouts, ground fine
3 eggs, beaten
1/4 cup tomato sauce
1/2 tsp salt
1/8 tsp pepper
1 tsp broth powder
1 Tbsp soy sauce or
  brown meat extract
1 egg, beaten

3/4 cup wheat germ
1/4 cup powdered milk
  (non-instant)
1/2 tsp sage
1/8 tsp thyme
2 Tbsp melted butter
3/4 cup fine dry bread
  crumbs
Bacon drippings or oil

Reserve 1 beaten egg, dry crumbs and bacon drippings. Combine the remaining ingredients and mix well to blend. Shape into the form of sausages. Roll in crumbs, then in beaten eggs and in crumbs again. Let stand 15 minutes to dry. Fry in bacon drippings or oil until brown. Mixture may also be made into sausage patties and placed on oiled baking sheet and baked in 350° oven for about 20 minutes. Serve plain or with tomato sauce for breakfast, luncheon or dinner. Makes 8 sausages 3 inches long.

Soy Sprouts Au Gratin

2 cups soy sprouts	2 Tbsp flour
1 cup grated sharp cheese	2 Tbsp butter
1/4 tsp salt	1 cup warm milk
1/8 tsp pepper	1 tsp prepared mustard
1 Tbsp grated onion	1/2 cup buttered bread
paprika	crumbs

Steam soy sprouts 20 minutes. Melt butter in saucepan, add flour and cook 1 minute. Remove from heat and gradually stir in milk. Return to heat and cook over low heat until it thickens, stirring constantly. Stir in 1/2 cup cheese, seasonings and soy sprouts. Pour into buttered casserole. Mix 1/2 cup cheese and buttered crumbs together and sprinkle over top. Sprinkle generously with paprika and bake in 350° oven for 30 minutes. Makes 4 servings.

Chicken Chow Mein

1 cup soy sprouts	1 cup mung bean sprouts
4 Tbsp oil	1 cup sliced onions
1/2 cup sliced celery	1/4 tsp salt
1 cup sliced canned	1/8 tsp pepper
mushrooms	1 Tbsp broth powder
1-1/2 cups diced cooked	seasoning
chicken	2 Tbsp cornstarch
2 Tbsp soy sauce	

Steam soy sprouts 15 minutes. Saute onions and celery in oil; add soy sprouts, mung bean sprouts, mushrooms and chicken. Measure liquid from mushrooms and add water to make 1 cup.

Combine with soy sauce and cornstarch and broth powder. Add to vegetables, bring to a boil and stir until thick. Add salt and pepper and cook covered for 5 minutes. Serve over cooked rice sprouts or Chinese noodles. Makes 4 servings.

Soy Sprout Burgers

2 cups ground, cooked 　soy sprouts	2 Tbsp minced onion
1 Tbsp broth seasoning	1/2 cup tomato sauce
1 Tbsp soy sauce	2 eggs, slightly beaten
1-1/2 cups wheat germ	1/2 tsp salt
1/8 tsp pepper	1/8 tsp chili powder

Combine eggs, tomato sauce, soy sauce, onion and seasonings. Stir in soy sprouts and wheat germ. Mix and let stand 15 minutes. Form into 8 patties and brown in hot oil or bacon drippings. Serve with brown gravy or tomato sauce or use with toasted hamburger buns, catsup, mustard, pickle, etc. One cup ground beef may be substituted for 1 cup of the soy sprouts, if desired. Makes 8 patties.

Soy Cheese Casserole

2 cups ground, cooked 　soy sprouts	1/2 cup buttered crumbs
3/4 cup chopped onions	2 Tbsp oil
1/2 tsp salt	3/4 cup thinly sliced celery
1/2 tsp broth powder	1/8 tsp pepper
1 cup drained, cooked 　tomatoes	1 cup grated sharp cheese
	1/2 cup tomato sauce

Saute celery and onions in oil. Add remaining ingredients, except crumbs. Mix to blend and pour into buttered casserole. Top with buttered crumbs and bake in 325° oven for 45 minutes. Makes 4 servings.

Chop Suey

2 cups mung bean sprouts	1 cup cooked chicken or
3/4 cup green pepper 　strips	pork, diced
	3/4 cup sliced onion

1 cup sliced celery	1 cup hot chicken broth
2 Tbsp cornstarch	1/4 cup cold water
1 tsp salt	1/8 tsp pepper
2 Tbsp soy sauce	2 cups cooked rice sprouts

Heat oil in heavy skillet and saute onions, pepper, and celery for 1 minute. Add chicken and saute 1 minute longer, stirring constantly. Add hot broth and bean sprouts, cover and cook 3 minutes. Combine cold water, cornstarch, soy sauce, salt and pepper and stir into hot mixture. Cook three minutes or until thick and smooth. Serve over hot cooked rice sprouts.

Variation: Substitute 1 cup soy sprouts for 1 cup mung sprouts. Steam them 20 minutes before adding. Makes 4 servings.

Chicken-Sprout Tostados

1 cup alfalfa sprouts	1 cup mung bean sprouts
1 pkg taco seasoning mix (1-1/4 oz.)	1-1/2 cups cooked chicken, shredded
3/4 cup sliced ripe olives	1 cup grated cheddar cheese
8 tortillas	2 cups seasoned pinto beans or refried beans
2 chopped tomatoes	
1 cup water	1 cup chopped green onions
oil for frying	1/2 cup sour cream

Combine taco mix with water and stir until dissolved. Heat to boiling, reduce heat and simmer 5 minutes. Add chicken and olives and simmer 2 minutes. Heat oil in large skillet and fry tortillas until crisp on both sides. Drain on paper towels. Heat beans in small saucepan. To serve, spread beans over tortillas and top with chicken mixture. Arrange cheese, tomatoes, sprouts and onions over chicken. Top with a spoonful of sour cream. Makes 8 tostados.

Sprouted Rice Balls

2 cups rice sprouts	1 beaten egg
1 cup grated carrots	1/2 tsp salt
1/4 cup grated onion	1 cup dried wheat sprouts (finely ground)
1/8 tsp pepper	
4 Tbsp oil	1 beaten egg
1 cup lean ground beef	

Sauce:

1 cup tomato juice	1/2 cup tomato sauce
1/4 tsp salt	1/8 tsp pepper
1/2 tsp chili powder	1/8 tsp garlic salt

Mix together the rice sprouts, meat, carrots, 1 egg, onion, salt and pepper. Form into 16 balls and roll in beaten egg and finely ground wheat sprouts. Brown in hot oil. Remove balls from skillet and add sauce ingredients. Mix well and bring to a boil. Return rice balls to skillet and simmer covered in the sauce for 30 minutes. Serve hot. Makes 4 servings.

Sprouted Wheat 'N' Cheese Loaf

2 cups sprouted wheat, coarsely ground	1 Tbsp minced onion
	1/8 tsp pepper
1 cup walnuts, chopped	1/4 cup milk
1/2 tsp salt	1 Tbsp Worcestershire sauce
2 Tbsp melted butter	
1/4 tsp paprika	3/4 cup soft bread crumbs
1 Tbsp lemon juice	
1 cup grated cheese	2 eggs, beaten

Combine eggs, milk and seasonings. Add remaining ingredients and blend well. Turn into buttered baking dish and bake in 350° oven for 45 minutes. Makes 4 servings.

Sprout Stuffed Peppers

4 medium green peppers	1 cup cooked soy sprouts, ground
1 cup lean ground beef	
1/4 cup minced onion	1 Tbsp oil
1/4 cup tomato sauce	1/4 cup minced celery
1/4 tsp salt	dash Tabasco sauce
1/8 tsp oregano	1/8 tsp pepper
1/2 cup fine dry bread crumbs	1/2 cup grated cheese

Cut peppers in half and remove seeds from inside. Boil 3 minutes, drain and keep hot. Brown meat in oil, but do not cook well done. Add onions, celery, seasonings, sprouts and tomato sauce. Blend together and fill hot pepper halves with mixture. Top with grated cheese and sprinkle dry crumbs over cheese. Place in baking pan and bake uncovered in 375° oven 15 minutes. Makes 8 pepper halves or 4 to 6 servings.

Sprout Stuffed Baked Tomatoes

4 large round, firm tomatoes	1 cup cooked soy sprouts, ground
1 cup lean ground beef	1 Tbsp oil
1/4 cup minced onion	1/4 cup minced celery
1/2 cup tomato pulp	dash Tabasco sauce
1/2 tsp salt	1/8 tsp pepper
1/8 tsp oregano	1/2 tsp chili pepper
1/8 tsp garlic salt	1/2 cup grated cheese
1/2 cup fine dry bread crumbs	

Cut slice from top of tomato and scoop out pulp. Turn upside down to drain while making filling. Brown meat in oil, but do not cook hard. Add onions, celery, seasonings, sprouts and tomato pulp. Blend together and fill tomatoes. Top with grated cheese and sprinkle dry crumbs over cheese. Place in baking pan and bake uncovered in 375° oven 20 minutes. Makes 4 servings.

Sprout Stuffed Eggplant

1 medium eggplant	1 Tbsp oil
1 cup lean ground beef	1/4 cup minced celery
1/4 cup minced onion	dash Tabasco sauce
1/2 cup tomato sauce	1/8 tsp pepper
1/2 tsp salt	1 cup grated cheese
1/8 tsp oregano	1 cup fine dry bread crumbs
1/2 tsp chili powder	
1/8 tsp garlic salt	1 Tbsp soy sauce
1 cup cooked soy sprouts, ground	

Cut eggplant in half and steam 15 minutes. Scoop out inside leaving a half inch around the outside. Chop the removed portion and reserve. Brown meat in oil, but do not cook until hard. Add onions, celery, seasonings, sprouts and tomato sauce. Stir in the reserved pulp. Pile into the two eggplant halves and top with the grated cheese and then with the crumbs. Place in baking pan and bake uncovered in 375° oven 20 to 25 minutes. Makes 6 servings.

Sprout Stuffed Cabbage Leaves

8 large cabbage leaves
1 cup lean ground beef
1/4 cup minced onion
1/4 cup tomato sauce
1/4 tsp salt
1/4 tsp oregano
1/8 tsp garlic salt
1 cup cooked soy sprouts,
    ground

1 Tbsp oil
1/4 cup minced celery
dash Tabasco sauce
1/8 tsp pepper
1/2 tsp chili powder
1 cup grated cheese

Brown meat in oil, but do not cook until hard. Add onions, celery, seasonings, sprouts and tomato sauce. Blend together and stir in the grated cheese. Dip the cabbage leaves in hot water, fill the centers with the meat mixture. Fold over and pin with toothpick. Place in buttered casserole and pour sauce over them. Cover and bake in 375° oven 25 minutes. Remove to hot serving dish and pour sauce over cabbage leaves. Makes 8 stuffed cabbage leaves or 4 to 6 servings.

Sauce for Cabbage Leaves:

2 cups tomato juice
1 Tbsp Worcestershire
    sauce
1/2 tsp onion salt
2 Tbsp cornstarch

2 Tbsp soy sauce
1 tsp sugar
1/8 tsp pepper
1/4 cup water

Combine all ingredients except cornstarch and water. Heat to boiling and thicken with cornstarch and water. Pour over cabbage leaves before baking.

Lima Bean Sprout Roast

2 cups lima bean sprouts,
   steamed 20 minutes
1 cup roasted peanuts,
   ground
1/4 cup milk
1 tsp salt

1/8 tsp garlic salt
2 cups mashed potatoes,
   seasoned
1 beaten egg
1/8 tsp paprika
1 Tbsp grated onion

Butter a baking dish and place a layer of potatoes in the bottom, then a layer of beans and a layer of peanuts. Repeat with second layer. Blend milk, egg and seasonings and pour over the top. Bake in a 350° oven 35 minutes. Makes 4 servings.

Boston Sprout Roast

3 cups sprouted kidney
   beans, steamed 30
   minutes
1-1/2 cups grated cheese
1 tsp salt
3 Tbsp minced onion
1/4 cup milk

2 beaten eggs
1/8 tsp pepper
1 cup whole wheat bread
   crumbs
2 Tbsp butter and
   2 Tbsp hot water

Chop beans fine and combine with remaining ingredients. except butter and hot water. Add a little more milk if necessary. Pack into a buttered loaf pan. Combine butter and hot water and·pour over the top. Bake in 350° oven 30 minutes. Makes 4 to 6 servings.

Corned Beef and Lima Sprout Casserole

2 cups lima bean sprouts,
   cooked 30 minutes
1 can cream of mushroom
   soup
1 cup grated cheese

1/2 cup bacon sprout
   bits
1/2 cup canned milk
1/4 cup minced onion
12 oz. can corned beef

Chill corned beef and cut into cubes. Combine corned beef with all ingredients, except bacon sprout bits. Pour into buttered casserole and top with the soy bacon sprout bits. Bake in 400° oven for 20 minutes. Makes 4 servings.

Hot Tamale Pie

1 cup sprouted pinto beans, cooked 30 minutes	1/2 cup sliced ripe olives
	1/4 tsp pepper
1 cup sprouted corn, cooked 20 minutes	1 Tbsp oil
	1/2 cup chopped green pepper
1 lb. ground beef	
1/2 cup chopped onion	2 tsp chili powder
1-1/2 cups cooked tomatoes	paprika
	corn meal mush
1 tsp salt	1 cup grated cheese

Saute onion and green pepper in oil. Remove from skillet and brown beef. Drain off any fat in pan. Combine the onion, green pepper, tomatoes, corn sprouts, bean sprouts, olives, chili powder, salt and pepper and mix well. Line bottom and sides of shallow baking casserole with corn meal mush. Pour in meat mixture and top with thin layer of corn meal mush. Top with grated cheese and paprika. Bake in 375° oven 30 minutes. Makes 6 servings.

Corn Meal Mush:

1 cup cold water	1 cup corn meal
3 cups boiling water	1 tsp salt

Stir corn meal into cold water. Gradually add boiling water and stir until thick and smooth, cooking over low heat.

Baked Bean Balls

2 cups cooked mashed pinto bean sprouts	1/2 cup wheat germ
	3 Tbsp prepared horse radish
1 lb. lean ground beef	
1 beaten egg	1 tsp salt
1 tsp vinegar	1/8 tsp garlic salt
1/8 tsp pepper	4 Tbsp grated onion
1/2 tsp crushed basil	tomato sauce
2 Tbsp soy sauce	

Combine ground beef and mashed pinto bean sprouts. Mix beaten egg, horse radish, vinegar and soy sauce together and add the seasonings and wheat germ. Combine with the meat mixture and blend together. Form into 24 balls. Place on oiled baking sheet and bake in 375° oven for about 20 minutes until brown. Place in serving dish and pour tomato sauce over bean balls to serve. Makes 6 servings.

Tomato Sauce:

1 can tomato soup   1/2 cup water
1/2 tsp chili powder

Combine all ingredients and simmer 5 minutes. Serve over baked bean balls.

Western Pinto Bean Sprouts

3 cups pinto bean sprouts   1 cup water
1 cup thinly sliced onion   1 clove garlic thinly
1 bay leaf   sliced
1/4 lb. ham or slab bacon   1/2 tsp salt
1/4 cup chopped green   1-1/2 cups cooked
   pepper   tomatoes
1 tsp chili powder   1 Tbsp brown sugar
1/4 tsp crushed oregano   1/4 tsp dry mustard

Cook bean sprouts in water for 30 minutes. Cut bacon or ham in 1-inch pieces and add to beans along with the remaining ingredients. Bring to boil, cover and simmer for 1 hour, stirring occasionally. Liquid on beans should be consistency of medium thick sauce. Serve hot in soup plates. Makes 6 servings.

Rancho Baked Bean Sprouts

4 cups pinto bean   2 cups water
   sprouts   1/8 tsp pepper
1 Tbsp dry mustard   1/4 cup brown sugar
1 tsp salt   1/2 cup chopped onion
1/4 cup molasses   1 tsp Worcestershire
3 Tbsp vinegar with   sauce
   pinch of cinnamon   1 cup diced ham
   and cloves

Cook bean sprouts in water 30 minutes. Add remaining ingredients, stir to mix and pour into bean pot or casserole. Cover and bake in 325° oven for 1-1/2 hours. Uncover and bake 30 minutes longer. Makes 8 servings.

Sprouted Pinto Bean Loaf

1/2 lb. ground beef	2 cups mashed, cooked
1/4 cup chopped onion	pinto bean sprouts
2 Tbsp chopped sweet	2 Tbsp chopped olives
pickle	1 beaten egg
1 cup tomato sauce	1/2 tsp salt
1/2 cup wheat germ	1/8 tsp pepper

Combine all ingredients and mix well. Pack into buttered loaf pan and bake in 350° oven for 1 hour. Serve plain or with tomato sauce. Makes 4 to 6 servings.

Bean Sprout Chili Deluxe

4 cups pinto bean sprouts	1 Tbsp oil
1 lb. ground beef (chuck)	1 clove garlic, chopped
1 cup chopped onion	1/2 cup chopped green
1 tsp salt	pepper
1/4 tsp ground pepper	2 tsp chili powder
1 Tbsp brown sugar	(more to taste)
3 cups cooked tomatoes	1/4 tsp hot pepper sauce
1/4 tsp cumin seed	1 tsp oregano, crumbled
2 cups water	1 Tbsp vinegar

Cook bean sprouts in water 30 minutes. Saute meat in the oil until lightly browned. Remove meat and add to beans. Pour off all except 1 Tbsp fat and saute onion, garlic and green pepper for about 3 minutes. Add to beans along with the remaining ingredients. Stir and bring to boil, turn to simmer and cover. Simmer 1 hour, stirring occasionally. Makes 8 servings.

Savory Baked Soybean Sprouts

4 cups sprouted soybeans	3 cups water
1 cup cooked tomatoes	1 cup diced tart apple
1/2 cup diced onion	2 tsp dry mustard

1 clove garlic
1 Tbsp cider vinegar
1/8 tsp pepper
1/2 lb. bacon cut into
   1-inch pieces

1/4 cup molasses
1 tsp salt
1/4 cup catsup

Cook soybeans in water 45 minutes. Add remaining ingredients, stir to mix and pour into bean pot or casserole. Cover and bake in 300° oven for 2 hours. Uncover and bake 30 minutes longer. If beans get too dry, add boiling water during baking period. Makes 8 servings.

Southern Baked Lima Sprouts

4 cups baby lima beans,
   sprouted
2 cups diced, unpeeled,
   tart apples
1/4 cup dark brown sugar
1/4 cup molasses
1/4 tsp black pepper

2 cups water
1/2 cup chopped onion
1/4 cup Worcestershire
   sauce
1 tsp salt
1/2 lb. slab bacon,
   diced

Cook bean sprouts in water for 30 minutes. Pour into bean pot or casserole and stir in remaining ingredients. Add enough boiling water to cover beans about half an inch. Cover and bake in 325° oven for 2 hours. Stir occasionally and add more boiling water if necessary. Bake uncovered for the last half hour. Makes 8 servings.

CHAPTER XIV

RECIPES FOR SALADS

Picnic Potato Sprout Salad

1 cup lentil or mung sprouts	1/8 tsp pepper
2 hard cooked eggs sliced	3 cups cubed, cooked potatoes
1/2 cup thinly sliced celery	1/2 cup radish slices
2 Tbsp chopped onion	2 Tbsp chopped sweet pickle
2 Tbsp French dressing	1/2 cup mayonnaise
1/2 tsp sugar	1/2 tsp prepared mustard
	1/4 tsp salt

Combine potatoes, eggs, radishes, celery, pickle, onion and sprouts; mix lightly. Combine dressings, mustard, sugar, salt and pepper. Pour over potato mixture and mix lightly. Makes 6 servings.

Soy Bit Luncheon Salad

1 cup alfalfa sprouts	1 cup romaine or Boston lettuce
4 Tbsp watercress sprouts	2 oz. Roquefort cheese, crumbled
4 Tbsp radish sprouts	2 medium tomatoes, diced
2 hard cooked eggs, sliced	1 cup cooked chicken or turkey cut in julienne strips
1 avocado, diced	1 Tbsp minced chives
1 small cucumber, diced	twist of black pepper, freshly ground
2 Tbsp green olive slices	
1/2 cup soy bacon bits	
1/2 cup French dressing	
1 cup red leaf lettuce	
1 cup spinach leaves	

Tear lettuce and spinach into bite size pieces. Add all other ingredients except soy bits and black pepper. Toss lightly with salad dressing and serve on large plates garnished with black pepper and soy bacon bits. Makes 4 servings.

Tomato Cups for Salad

Select firm, ripe medium size tomatoes. Wash and cut off stem end. Carefully scoop out seeds and pulp, reserving for later use. Sprinkle inside with salt or celery salt, turn upside down and chill in refrigerator until serving time. Fill cups with favorite seafood, chicken, meat, cottage cheese or vegetable mixture.

Tomatoes with Mung Sprouts

1 cup mung bean sprouts	2 cups tomato pulp
2 Tbsp sliced green onion	(from above recipe)
2 Tbsp chopped green	2 Tbsp diced celery
pepper	1 tsp sugar
1/2 tsp salt	1/8 tsp ground pepper
1/2 cup grated cheddar	1/4 tsp chili powder
cheese	

Mix all ingredients together except cheese. Chill well. At serving time spoon into individual bowls and sprinkle with grated cheese. This is a good side dish to serve with hot or cold meats, baked fish, tamales, etc. Two cups cold canned tomatoes may also be used. Makes 4 servings.

Lentil Stuffed Tomatoes

1 cup lentil sprouts	4 medium firm ripe
2 Tbsp cress sprouts	tomatoes
1/2 cup shredded carrot	1/2 cup sliced celery
1/2 cup cubed sharp	1/4 cup sliced ripe olives
cheddar cheese	1/3 cup mayonnaise

Cut off stem end of tomatoes and scoop out seeds and pulp. Sprinkle with celery salt inside, turn upside down and chill in refrigerator. Combine remaining ingredients and fill tomato cups. Sprinkle tops with the cress sprouts. Makes 4 servings.

Surprise Egg Salad

2 cups alfalfa sprouts	4 hard cooked eggs,
4 oz. Swiss cheese cut	coarsely chopped
in slivers	1/2 cup mayonnaise

1 cup mung sprouts
1/4 cup chopped green
  pepper
1/2 tsp salt
paprika

1 Tbsp mustard with
  horse radish
2 Tbsp chopped pimiento
1/8 tsp pepper

Combine all ingredients except alfalfa sprouts and paprika. Toss lightly to coat. Chill well and serve on bed of alfalfa sprouts and garnish with paprika. Makes 4 servings.

Chicken Mung Salad

1/2 cup mung sprouts
2 Tbsp cress sprouts
2 Tbsp sliced ripe olives
1/2 cup sliced celery
3/4 cup mayonnaise
salt & pepper to taste
2 cups cubed cooked
  chicken

2 Tbsp sliced green
  olives
2 Tbsp pickle relish
2 hard cooked eggs,
  sliced
paprika
1/2 cup toasted soy
  sprouts

Combine all ingredients and toss lightly. Serve on crisp lettuce. Garnish with paprika and cress sprouts or use to stuff avocados or tomatoes. Makes 6 servings.

Frankfurter Lentil Salad

3/4 cup lentil sprouts
1 cup cooked, diced
  potatoes
2 Tbsp chopped green
  pepper
1/4 cup chili sauce
1/8 tsp pepper

4 cooked, sliced
  frankfurters
1/2 cup sliced green
  onion with tops
2 tsp prepared mustard
1/4 tsp salt
1/4 cup chopped cucumber

Combine frankfurters, potatoes and lentil sprouts. Mix remaining ingredients and blend. Pour over salad mixture and toss lightly. Serve on bed of lettuce, cress or alfalfa sprouts. Makes 4 servings.

Crunchy Stuffed Avocado

1/2 cup lentil sprouts
1/4 cup thinly sliced celery

1 6-1/2 oz. can tuna fish
4 Tbsp mayonnaise

3 Tbsp lemon juice
2 Tbsp sliced green onions
paprika

1/4 cup toasted soy sprouts
    chopped
2 avocados

Wash and cut avocados in half lengthwise. Hollow out slightly to make larger cavity for filling and sprinkle with lemon juice. Combine tuna, celery, lentil sprouts, soy sprouts, onions, 2 Tbsp lemon juice and extra avocado. Heap into a mound in the avocado shell halves and sprinkle with paprika. Serve in lettuce cups. Makes 4 servings.

Corned Beef and Lentil Salad

1 cup lentil sprouts
1/2 cup sliced cucumber
4 green onions sliced
1/4 tsp salt
1/8 tsp ground pepper
3/4 cup sour cream
1 Tbsp lemon juice

1 cup cubed corned canned
    beef (chill first for easy
    cutting)
1/2 cup sliced radishes
2 tomatoes cut into wedges
1/8 tsp celery salt

Combine sour cream and lemon juice. Combine remaining ingredients and pour the sour cream over them. Toss lightly. Serve in lettuce cups. Makes 4 servings.

Chef's Sprout Potato Salad

1 cup mung bean sprouts
2 cups diced cooked potatoes
1/2 cup diced celery
1/2 tsp salt
2 hard cooked eggs sliced
2 Tbsp minced parsley
3/4 cup yogurt salad dressing

1 cup canned pork-ham
    luncheon meat cubed
1/2 cup diced American
    cheese
1/4 cup sliced green onions
1/8 tsp garlic salt
paprika

Combine all ingredients except egg slices and parsley. Mix to coat with salad dressing. Pour into serving bowl and garnish with egg slices and parsley. Sprinkle egg yolks with paprika. Chill in refrigerator at least 2 hours for flavors to blend. Makes 4 servings.

Pea Sprouts with Macaroni and Cheese

1 cup steamed pea sprouts, chilled	1 cup cooked chilled macaroni
2 cups alfalfa sprouts	1 cup cubed sharp cheddar cheese
1/2 cup thinly sliced celery	
2 Tbsp chopped green pepper	2 Tbsp sliced green onions
2 Tbsp yogurt	1/2 cup mayonnaise
salt & pepper to taste	1 tsp curry powder

Combine pea sprouts, macaroni, cheese, celery, onions and green pepper. Mix mayonnaise, yogurt and curry powder together and pour over salad. Salt and pepper to taste. Toss lightly. Serve on bed of alfalfa sprouts. Makes 4 servings.

Tunapple Mung Salad

1 cup mung bean sprouts	1 can solid pack white tuna (6-1/2 oz.)
1 cup drained pineapple chunks	
	1/2 cup walnuts
1 cup lettuce, bite size pieces	1/2 cup thinly sliced celery
1 Tbsp lemon juice	1/4 cup sour cream
1/2 cup mayonnaise	2 Tbsp sugar
paprika	

Flake the tuna and combine with pineapple, celery, mung sprouts and lettuce and walnuts. Combine remaining ingredients and toss all together. Serve in lettuce cups garnished with paprika. Makes 4 servings.

Garbanzo Country Salad

2 cups garbanzo sprouts (steamed & chilled)	8 oz. cheese, chilled & diced
	2 hard cooked eggs, sliced
2 cups alfalfa sprouts	1/2 cup salad oil
1 cup thinly sliced onions, separate into rings	2 Tbsp cider vinegar
	1 tsp vegetable seasoning
2 Tbsp lemon juice	1/2 tsp dill seed

Combine garbanzo sprouts, cheese and onion slices in bowl. Mix oil, lemon juice, vinegar, vegetable seasoning and dill seed together. Pour over garbanzo mixture and toss lightly. Place on beds of alfalfa sprouts and garnish with egg slices. Makes 4 servings.

Tomato-Shrimp Aspic

2 cups alfalfa sprouts	1 Tbsp unflavored gelatin
1 tsp grated onion	2 cups tomato juice
1/2 tsp salt	1 Tbsp sugar or honey
1 Tbsp Worcestershire sauce	2 Tbsp vinegar
1/2 tsp celery seed	2 Tbsp lemon juice
1/2 cup thinly sliced celery	1 8 oz. can small shrimp
1 cup mung sprouts, chopped	

Soften gelatin in 1/2 cup tomato juice. Heat remaining tomato juice and dissolve gelatin in it. Add salt, sugar, and seasonings and chill, but do not let it set. Fold in celery, mung sprouts and shrimp. Pour into oiled mold and refrigerate until set. Unmold on bed of alfalfa sprouts and serve with yogurt salad dressing.

Jellied Vegetables and Lentil Sprouts

3/4 cup lentil sprouts	1 Tbsp unflavored gelatin
1/4 cup cold water	1/4 cup boiling water
1/2 tsp salt	1/4 cup sugar or honey
1/4 cup lemon juice	1/4 cup vinegar
1/4 cup grated onion	3/4 cup shredded cabbage
2 Tbsp minced green pepper	1/2 cup coarsley grated
1/2 cup chopped celery	carrots
1/4 cup sliced stuffed olives	

Soften gelatin in 1/4 cup cold water. Dissolve in boiling water. Add salt, sugar, lemon juice, vinegar and stir to dissolve sugar. Chill until it begins to thicken. Add remaining ingredients and pour into oiled molds or shallow pan. Unmold on bed of lettuce, cress or alfalfa sprouts. Serve with quick Russian dressing. Makes 6 servings.

Lentil Relish Molds

3/4 cup lentil sprouts	1 envelope unflavored
1/4 cup cold water	gelatin
1/2 tsp salt	1/4 cup boiling water
1/2 cup sour cream or yogurt	1/2 cup mayonnaise

2 Tbsp sliced stuffed olives
1/2 cup pickle relish
1/2 cup finely diced cucumber
dash tabasco
1/2 cup celery

1 Tbsp prepared mustard
1 Tbsp grated onion
1/4 cup minced green
pepper

Soften gelatin in cold water. Add boiling water and stir over low heat until gelatin is completely dissolved. Cool and stir in remaining ingredients. Pour into 6 individual molds and chill until set. Unmold on bed of lettuce, alfalfa sprouts or cress. Serve with assorted cold cuts. Makes 6 servings.

Cucumber Combo

3/4 cup chopped mung
  sprouts
1-1/2 cup hot water
1 Tbsp horseradish
1 Tbsp grated onion
1/2 cup mayonnaise

1 pkg lemon jello
1 tsp vinegar
1/4 tsp salt
3/4 cup ground or grated
  cucumber

Dissolve jello in hot water. Cool and let stand in refrigerator until of egg white consistency. Add remaining ingredients and mix thoroughly. Pour into 8 x 8 square pan or individual molds. Chill until firm. Unmold on bed of salad greens. Serve with yogurt dressing or sour cream dressing. Makes 6 servings.

Green Salad Mold

1 cup alfalfa sprouts chopped
1 cup hot water
1/4 tsp salt
1 Tbsp lemon juice
1/2 cup sliced green onions
  with tops

1 pkg lime gelatin
1 cup cold water
1 ripe avocado, mashed
1/2 cup thinly sliced
  radishes
1 cup shredded cabbage

Dissolve gelatin in hot water. Stir in cold water and salt. Chill until it begins to thicken. Stir lemon juice into mashed avocado and blend with gelatin. Fold in remaining ingredients. Pour into mold and chill until firm. Makes 6 servings.

Oriental Bean Sprout Salad

2 cups mung sprouts
2 cups lettuce, bite size
  pieces
2 Tbsp sesame seeds

1/2 cup sliced fresh
  mushrooms (or drained
  canned)
1/2 tsp dry mustard

Dressing:
1/2 tsp seasoned salt
1/8 garlic powder

1/4 cup oil
1/4 cup vinegar

Mix dressing and chill. Combine lettuce, sprouts and mushrooms and toss lightly with dressing. Sprinkle with sesame seeds and serve immediately. Makes 6 servings.

Bean Sprout Salad

1 cup kidney bean sprouts,
  steamed & cooled
1 cup garbanzo beans,
  steamed & cooled
1 cup cut green beans,
  cooked
1 green pepper cut in rings

1/2 cup oil
1/2 cup vinegar
1 tsp mustard seed
1/2 tsp garlic salt
1 large onion cut in rings
2 Tbsp sugar

Heat vinegar and dissolve sugar, salt and mustard. Add oil and mustard seed and cool. Combine bean sprouts, green pepper and onion. Pour dressing over bean sprouts and toss lightly. Chill 24 hours before serving. Makes 6 servings.

Wilted Lettuce with Mung Sprouts

1 cup mung bean sprouts
1/4 cup vinegar
1/4 tsp salt
4 cups leaf lettuce, red
2 cups spinach leaves

4 slices bacon
6 sliced green onions with
  tops
1/8 tsp pepper

Saute bacon until crisp. Remove from pan and break into small pieces. To the drippings, add the vinegar and sliced onions and heat to boiling point. Combine the lettuce, spinach and mung sprouts and pour the hot sauce over them. Toss lightly to coat all leaves. Season with salt and pepper and serve at once. Makes 4 servings.

Lentil Sprout Slaw

1 cup lentil sprouts
1/4 cup pimiento
2 Tbsp vinegar
1/2 cup sour cream
Salt and pepper to taste

3 cups slivered cabbage
1-1/2 Tbsp sugar
2 Tbsp mayonnaise
2 Tbsp liquid from pimiento

Sliver cabbage with very sharp knife and mix with lentil sprouts. Combine remaining ingredients for dressing and pour over cabbage sprout mixture. Toss to mix and serve immediately. Makes 4 servings.

Mandarin-Mung Slaw

1 cup mung bean sprouts
1 can mandarin oranges
  drained
1 avocado, halved and sliced
  in 1/2" slices

3 cups slivered cabbage
1/2 cup ripe, pitted olives

Dressing:
1/2 cup mayonnaise
1 Tbsp lemon juice

1 Tbsp mandarin orange
  juice
Combine and chill

Combine cabbage, bean sprouts and olives and toss with one half the dressing. Divide into four individual salad bowls or plates and arrange orange and avocado slices alternately around outer edge of salad. Drizzle remaining dressing over oranges and avocado. Makes 4 servings.

Stuffed Lettuce with Sprouts

1/2 cup lentil sprouts
1/2 cup mung bean sprouts
2 Tbsp blue cheese
1 Tbsp minced green pepper
1 Tbsp minced pimiento
1/4 cup mayonnaise
twist black pepper
dash paprika

1 large head lettuce
1 3-oz. cream cheese
2 Tbsp grated carrot
2 Tbsp diced tomato
1 Tbsp minced chives or
  onion
1/8 tsp salt

Cut center from head of lettuce and save for future use. Soften cheese and blend with mayonnaise. Stir in remaining ingredients and mix well. Pack into hollow head of lettuce. Wrap in damp cloth and chill for 2 hours or more. Slice crosswise for individual servings. Serve with yogurt mayonnaise or sour cream dressing. Makes 6 servings.

Spinach Sprout Salad

2 cups torn spinach leaves	2 cups red leaf lettuce
1 cup mung bean sprouts	1 cup alfalfa sprouts
1/2 cup sliced cucumbers	1/2 cup sliced green onions

Combine chilled greens in large salad bowl. Add remaining ingredients and toss lightly to mix. Serve with Milbourne Dressing or any favorite salad dressing. Makes 6 servings.

Sprout Salad Bowl

2 cups alfalfa sprouts	1 cup mung bean sprouts
1/2 cup lentil sprouts	4 Tbsp watercress sprouts
2 cups Boston lettuce	1/2 cup sliced green onions
1/2 cup sliced cucumbers	1 large avocado, diced
2 medium tomatoes, diced	1/4 cup coarsely grated carrots

Combine all ingredients in large salad bowl. Toss lightly to mix. Chill until serving time. Serve with Green Mayonnaise or dressing of choice. Dressing may be added to salad just before serving and tossed lightly, or pass dressing separately with salad. Makes 6 large servings.

Soy Waldorf Salad

2 cups alfalfa sprouts	2 cups apple
2 cups celery	1 cup soy nuts chopped
1/2 cup raisins	1/4 cup mayonnaise
1/4 cup yogurt	1/2 tsp sugar
1/2 tsp cider vinegar	paprika

Combine apple, celery, nuts and raisins. Mix together mayonnaise, yogurt, sugar and vinegar. Pour over apple mixture and toss all together. Serve on bed of alfalfa sprouts. Garnish with paprika. Makes 6 servings.

CHAPTER XV

RECIPES FOR SALAD DRESSINGS

Yogurt Salad Dressing

2 cups yogurt
1 dash tobasco sauce
1/4 cup chili sauce or ketchup
1/2 tsp dill weed
1 Tbsp minced chives

1/4 cup mayonnaise
1 tsp Worcestershire sauce
1/4 tsp lemon pepper
1/4 tsp garlic powder
1 tsp sugar

Mix together and refrigerate 12 hours to blend flavors. Will keep well in refrigerator for two weeks. Serve with green salads or as a dip with fresh vegetable sticks. Makes 2-1/2 cups.

Tartar Sauce

1 cup yogurt salad dressing
1 Tbsp finely chopped green
  onion with tops

1 tsp dijon mustard
1 Tbsp finely chopped
  sweet pickle

Combine and serve with fish. Makes 1 cup.

Special Slaw Dressing

1 cup sour cream
4 Tbsp vinegar

4 Tbsp mayonnaise
3 Tbsp sugar

Combine all ingredients and chill. Makes 1-1/4 cups.

Blue Cheese Dressing

1 cup sour cream
2 Tbsp grated onion
1 tsp lemon juice
2 oz. blue cheese

1 cup mayonnaise
2 Tbsp cider vinegar
1/8 tsp salt
twist ground black pepper

Freeze blue cheese and grate on coarse grater. Combine all ingredients and chill before serving. Keeps 2 weeks in refrigerator. Yogurt may be substituted for half or all of the sour cream to reduce calories. Makes 2-1/2 cups.

Sour Cream Dressing

3/4 cup sour cream   3 Tbsp lemon juice
4 Tbsp vinegar   1/4 tsp salt
2 Tbsp sugar

Combine and chill before serving over salad. Makes 1 cup.

French Dressing

1 can condensed tomato soup   1/2 cup sugar
1 cup salad oil   1 Tbsp dry mustard
1/2 tsp paprika   1 Tbsp grated onion
1 Tbsp Worcestershire sauce   1/2 tsp pepper
2/3 cup vinegar

Put all ingredients in jar except vinegar and shake well. Add vinegar and shake again. Store in refrigerator. Makes 3 cups.

Blender Mayonnaise

2 eggs   1 Tbsp cider vinegar
1 Tbsp honey   1 Tbsp lemon juice
1/8 tsp salt   2 cups oil, chilled (approx.)

Be sure that all ingredients are chilled. Beat eggs in blender 30 seconds. Add vinegar, lemon juice, honey and salt and blend 30 seconds longer. Turn blender to low and remove small cover and slowly add oil until mixture is thick. It may not be necessary to use all of the oil. If necessary, stop blender a time or two and stir mayonnaise with rubber spatula while adding oil. Store in tightly covered jar in refrigerator. The amount of vinegar, honey, lemon juice and salt may be increased or decreased to suit individual tastes. Makes 2 cups.

Green Mayonnaise

1 cup blender mayonnaise   4 Tbsp chopped spinach
1 tsp dried tarragon leaves 4 Tbsp watercress
1/8 tsp garlic salt   4 Tbsp parsley
twist of black pepper   4 Tbsp water

Cook spinach, watercress and parsley in water 2 minutes. Cool and puree in blender with 2 Tbsp cooking liquid and tarragon leaves. Add green puree, garlic salt and pepper to mayonnaise and stir to blend. Serve on green salads, chicken or fish salads. Makes 1-1/2 cups mayonnaise.

Quick Russian Dressing

1/2 cup mayonnaise   3 Tbsp yogurt
3 Tbsp chili sauce

Combine all ingredients and mix well. Makes 3/4 cup.

Old-Fashioned Salad Dressing

1/4 cup sugar   1/2 cup vinegar
1/2 tsp salt   1 tsp mustard
1/4 cup flour   1 tall can evaporated milk
3 slightly-beaten eggs   1/2 cup water

Mix sugar, salt, and flour; add eggs, water, vinegar and mustard. Cook in double boiler until thick, stirring constantly. Chill. Add chilled evaporated milk. Beat until light and fluffy. Makes 2 cups.

Melbourne Dressing

2/3 cup lemon juice   1/4 cup salad oil or olive oil
1/4 cup Worcestershire sauce 3 Tbsp sugar

Cover jar tightly and shake vigorously to blend well. Store in covered container in refrigerator. Shake well before using. Makes 1-1/4 cups.

CHAPTER XVI

RECIPES FOR SOUPS

Cream of Corn Soup

2 cups corn sprouts	1 cup boiling water
4 Tbsp minced onion	3 Tbsp butter
2 Tbsp flour	1-1/4 cup chicken stock
1-1/4 cup milk	2 Tbsp minced pimiento
1/2 tsp salt	1/8 tsp ground pepper
1/2 cup cream or canned milk	1 Tbsp chopped chives

Grind corn sprouts and cook in boiling water 20 minutes. While corn is cooking, saute onion in butter until transparent. Remove pan from heat and stir in flour. Cook 1 minute. Add corn, undrained, chicken stock, milk and cook 5 minutes, stirring constantly. Add salt and pepper, pimientos and cream. Blend and heat but do not boil. Sprinkle chives over soup to serve. Makes 4 servings.

Vegetable Beef Soup

1/2 cup lentil sprouts	3/4 lb boneless beef
1/2 cup pea sprouts	1/2 cup canned tomatoes
1/2 cup chopped onion	1/2 cup sliced carrots
1/2 cup sliced celery	1/2 cup cubed potatoes
4 cups beef broth	1 tsp salt
1/8 tsp pepper	2 Tbsp oil
1 cup water	

Cut beef into 3/4 inch cubes and cook in oil until brown on all sides. Add 1 cup water, cover and simmer 1 to 2 hours or tender. Add beef broth, and all vegetables, except lentils. Cover and simmer 20 minutes. Add salt, pepper and lentil sprouts and cook 5 minutes longer. Makes 6 servings.

Pinto Bean Soup

3 cups sprouted pinto beans	3 cups water
1 cup diced ham	2 bouillon cubes
1 cup chopped onions	1/2 cup diced celery
1/2 cup diced carrots	1 cup tomato sauce
1 can tomato soup	1 tsp salt
1/8 tsp pepper	1 Tbsp Worcestershire sauce

Cook sprouted beans in water for 1 hour. Remove two cups of beans from saucepan and mash. Reserve for later. Add remaining ingredients, bring to boil and cook on low heat, covered, for another hour. Add mashed beans and cook 15 minutes, stirring occasionally. If soup is too thick, add a little hot water and adjust seasonings. Makes 4 servings.

Soy Clam Chowder

1 cup soy sprouts	1 can minced clams
1 cup diced potatoes	(6-1/2 oz.)
1/2 cup chopped celery	1/2 cup chopped onions
3/4 cup water	1/2 cup water
1 cup cream or canned milk	1 cup milk
4 Tbsp butter	2 Tbsp flour
1/8 tsp pepper	1/2 tsp salt
1/16 tsp thyme	

Cook soy sprouts in 1/2 cup water 30 minutes and puree smooth in blender. Drain clams and combine liquid with 3/4 cup water, potatoes, celery and onions and cook 20 minutes or until tender. In another pan melt butter and slowly add flour, salt, pepper and thyme. Gradually add the milk, cream and any water remaining on cooked vegetables. Cook until thick and smooth. Stir in pureed soy beans and clams and heat but do not boil. Makes 4 servings.

Sprouted Vegetable Soup

1/2 cup Alaskan pea sprouts	1 cup coarsely ground
1/2 lb ground beef	cooked soy sprouts
1 small colve garlic chopped	1/2 cup chopped onion
1/2 cup carrots sliced	1/2 cup sliced celery

3 cups beef stock
1 tsp salt
1 Tbsp Worcestershire
sauce

1 cup canned tomatoes
2 bouillon cubes
1/8 tsp pepper

Brown meat and break into small pieces while cooking. Add onions and garlic and cook 1 minute. Add remaining ingredients, cover and simmer 30 minutes. Makes 6 servings.

Chicken-Rice Soup

1 cup diced, cooked
chicken
1 cup rice sprouts
4 green onions, sliced
1/4 cup finely diced
celery
1/2 tsp salt
1/4 cup drained, canned
tomatoes, chopped

4 cups chicken stock
2 chicken bouillon
cubes
1/4 cup finely diced
carrots
1/2 cup fresh or frozen
green peas
1/8 tsp pepper
1 Tbsp minced parsley

Heat chicken stock and add bouillon cubes and rice and cook 20 minutes. Add remaining ingredients except parsley and simmer another 20 minutes. Sprinkle with parsley and serve hot. Makes 4 servings.

Minestrone with Sprouts

1/2 cup pea sprouts
1/2 cup rice sprouts
1/2 cup navy bean or
lima sprouts
1 garlic bud, chopped
2 cups canned tomatoes
1/2 cup diced celery
1/2 cup sliced or diced
carrots
2 Tbsp minced parsley
1/4 tsp ground pepper
1/8 tsp oregano

Parmesan cheese
4 strips bacon, diced
1/4 lb. ham, diced
1 cup chopped onion
4 cups beefstock
1/4 cup tomato paste
1/2 cup shredded cabbage
1/2 cup sliced zucchini
1/4 tsp sage
salt to taste
1/2 cup sliced Italian
sausage

Fry bacon and diced ham. Add onion and garlic and cook until transparent. In large kettle combine beef stock, canned tomatoes, tomato paste, bacon, ham, onion, garlic, all vegetables and seasonings. Bring to boiling point, cover and simmer about 40 minutes or until thick. Add sliced sausage and serve as a main dish soup. Sprinkle with Parmesan cheese. Makes 6 servings.

Creole Bean Sprout Soup

2 cups adzuki bean sprouts	4 strips bacon cut in 1-inch pieces
4 Tbsp chopped onion	2 cups cooked tomatoes
2 cups beef stock	1 tsp vinegar
2 Tbsp grated horse-radish	1/8 tsp ground black pepper
1/2 tsp salt	
3 Tbsp chopped green pepper	

Cook beans in 1/2 cup water 15 minutes. Puree in blender. Fry bacon until crisp and remove from pan. Add onion and green pepper and saute until golden. Puree tomatoes in blender and combine all ingredients except horseradish. Simmer over low heat 15 minutes. Add vinegar and horseradish, mix well and serve hot with garlic flavored croutons. Makes 4 servings.

Soy Mushroom Soup

2 cups soy sprouts	1 cup water
1/2 lb. fresh mushrooms	4 Tbsp butter
1 tsp salt	1/8 tsp pepper
3 cups milk	1 cup cream or canned milk
paprika	

Cook soy sprouts in 1/2 cup water 30 minutes. Puree in blender. Clean mushrooms and cut into very small pieces and simmer in 1/2 cup water 15 minutes. Combine bean puree, mushrooms and cooking water, butter, salt, pepper, milk and cream. Stir and heat to boiling point, but do not boil. Serve and sprinkle with paprika. Makes 4 servings.

Lentil Sprout Soup

2 cups lentil sprouts	1/2 cup thinly sliced carrots
4 slices bacon	

1/4 cup diced green peppers	3/4 cup sliced onion
1/2 cup cooked tomatoes	2 Tbsp flour
1/2 tsp salt	1 Tbsp wine vinegar
1/4 tsp ground pepper	1/2 tsp oregano
3 cups beef or ham stock	

Simmer lentil sprouts in 1 cup stock. Cut bacon into small pieces and cook until crisp. Remove bacon from pan and measure out 2 Tbsp fat and reserve. Add all the vegetables to remaining bacon fat and saute over low heat 5 minutes. Remove vegetables and combine with lentils and bacon in saucepan. Put reserved 2 Tbsp bacon fat and flour in skillet and blend together and cook over low heat 1 minute. Remove from heat and stir in beef stock, salt and vinegar and pepper. Cook 1 minute and add to lentil mixture. Bring to boiling point, stirring constantly. Reduce heat and simmer covered 10 minutes, stirring frequently. Add black pepper and serve with croutons or crackers. Makes 4 servings.

Cream of Pea Sprout Soup

1-1/2 cups Alaskan pea sprouts	paprika
2 cups meat stock or bouillon	1/2 cup water
	2 cups milk
2 Tbsp flour	1/2 tsp salt
1/8 tsp pepper	2 Tbsp butter or bacon drippings
1/2 cup heavy cream or canned milk	2 strips crisp bacon, crumbled

Cook sprouts in 1/2 cup water 15 minutes or until tender. Blend them into a puree in blender. Mix flour with 1/4 cup stock. Combine with the remaining stock and milk. Stir and cook for about 6 minutes or until slightly thickened. Stir in pea puree, salt, pepper and butter. Heat, but do not boil. Stir in cream or canned milk just before serving. Garnish with crumbled bacon and paprika. Makes 6 servings.

Navy Bean Sprout Soup with Ham Balls

4 cups navy or lima bean sprouts	1/4 tsp pepper
	2 cups water

1 cup tomato juice
1 cup sliced onion
1/2 cup diced green
   pepper

1 cup tomato sauce
1/2 cup diced celery
1 tsp salt
1 Tbsp soy sauce

Cook bean sprouts in water 30 minutes. Add remaining ingredients and bring to boil. Turn heat down and simmer covered 1 hour. Add ham balls and simmer 30 minutes longer. Makes 6 servings.

Ham Balls

1-1/2 cups ground, cooked
   ham
1/2 tsp dry mustard
1/4 cup dried wheat sprouts,
   ground

1 slightly beaten
   egg
1/8 tsp pepper

Combine and drop into hot soup and simmer 30 minutes.

Cream of Soy Sprout Soup

2 cups cooked ground
   soy sprouts
1/2 cup chopped onion
1/2 tsp salt
dash cayenne
paprika

2-1/2 cups milk
1 Tbsp bacon fat
1/8 tsp pepper
4 strips crisp bacon,
   crumbled
1 Tbsp parsley

Saute onion in bacon fat until transparent. Pour 1-1/2 cups milk, soy sprouts and onion into blender and blend until smooth. Combine with remaining milk, salt, pepper and cayenne and heat in double boiler or over low heat, stirring to prevent sticking. Do not boil. Pour into serving bowls and garnish with crumbled bacon, paprika and parsley. Makes 4 servings.

French Soy-Onion Soup

1 cup cooked ground
   soy sprouts
3 cups bouillon or beef
   broth
1/2 tsp salt

1 Tbsp soy sauce
2 cups thinly sliced
   onions
2 Tbsp bacon fat
1/8 tsp pepper

Cook onions in bacon fat until golden brown. Blend soy sprouts, salt, pepper, soy sauce and bouillon until smooth. Pour into saucepan, add browned onions, including bacon drippings and heat to boiling. Let simmer 5 minutes. Serve with cheese croutons. Makes 4 servings.

Croutons for Soup

Cut stale bread (cracked wheat, whole wheat, sprouted wheat, or white, etc.) into slices about 1/3 of an inch thick. Remove crust if desired. Dry and roll into fine crumbs for future use. Spread slices of bread with butter, cut in cubes and bake in 350° oven until golden brown. Serve with soup.

CHAPTER XVII

RECIPES FOR VEGETABLES

Mandarin Vegetables

1 cup lentil sprouts	1/2 cup green beans,
1/2 cup almond sprouts	1 inch pieces
1/2 cup sliced green	1/2 cup sliced
onions	cauliflower
1 cup water	1 Tbsp soy sauce
2 chicken bouillon cubes	2 tsp cornstarch
1/8 tsp garlic salt	twist or two black
1/2 cup thinly sliced	pepper
carrots	

Heat oil in heavy skillet and stir-fry carrots and beans over medium heat for 2 minutes. Add cauliflower and onions and stir-fry 1 minute. Blend cornstarch into water and add, stirring until thick. Add chicken bouillon cubes, and stir until dissolved. Stir in lentil sprouts and almonds, bring to a boil and serve. Makes 6 servings.

Baked Pea Sprouts with Carrots

1-1/2 cups Alaskan	1-1/2 cups sliced carrots
pea sprouts	1/2 tsp salt
1/2 cup water	4 Tbsp butter
1 tsp lemon juice	1/2 tsp sugar
1 cup sliced onions	twist or two of black
1 Tbsp minced parsley	pepper

Cook pea sprouts and carrots in water 15 minutes. Drain and reserve the water. Arrange in buttered casserole, alternately with onion rings. Combine reserved cooking water, butter, lemon juice, sugar, salt and pepper and pour over vegetables. Cover and bake in 350° oven 30 minutes. Sprinkle with parsley to serve. Makes 6 servings.

Potato Crisp with Lentils

1 cup lentil sprouts	1/2 cup finely minced
3 cups grated raw potato,	onion
firmly packed	4 Tbsp butter
1/2 tsp salt	1/8 tsp pepper

Grate potatoes immediately before cooking to prevent turning brown. Combine potatoes, sprouts, onion, salt and pepper. Heat 2 Tbsp butter in heavy skillet until butter starts to brown. Pour in potato mixture and spread evenly in pan. Cover and cook over medium heat about 10 to 12 minutes or until crisp and brown on bottom. Remove from heat and cover with large plate, invert skillet and turn out on plate. Add remaining 2 Tbsp butter to skillet, heat until butter starts to brown. Carefully slide potatoes from plate into pan and cook uncovered about 10 minutes until other side is brown. Turn out onto serving plate and cut in wedges to serve. It is delicious with meat, fish or eggs. Makes 4 servings.

Spanish Corn Sprouts

2 cups corn sprouts	pinch chili powder
4 Tbsp chopped green	1/4 cup water
pepper	4 Tbsp diced pimiento
4 Tbsp sliced green onion	2 Tbsp butter

Cook corn in water 30 minutes. There should be no more than 1 Tbsp liquid remaining. Remove from heat and stir in remaining ingredients, cover and simmer 5 minutes. Makes 4 servings.

Green Beans and Corn Sprouts Parmesan

2 cups corn sprouts	2 cups cut green beans
1/4 cup grated onion	1 tsp celery seed
1/4 tsp salt	1/8 tsp pepper
2 Tbsp butter	1/4 cup Parmesan
paprika	cheese

Cook corn 30 minutes in 1/2 cup water. Cook green beans until almost done. Drain and reserve about 1 Tbsp liquid from each. In buttered casserole place a layer of beans and one of corn. Add onion and butter to liquid and pour half over corn. Sprinkle with half the salt, pepper and Parmesan cheese. Repeat with second layer. Bake in 400° oven 12 minutes. Sprinkle with paprika and serve hot. Makes 6 servings.

Double Beans Parmesan

1-1/2 cup mung bean sprouts	1-1/2 cup green beans, cut in 1-1/2 inch pieces
1/4 cup water	
1/4 cup salad oil	1/4 cup minced onion
1/2 tsp salt	1/4 cup wine vinegar
1/2 cup grated Parmesan cheese	1/3 tsp pepper

Cook green beans in 1/4 cup water until tender. Drain and combine with mung bean sprouts. Add remaining ingredients and toss lightly to evenly distribute dressing. Heat for one minute and serve. Makes 4 servings.

Savory Lentil Sprouts and New Potatoes

1 cup lentil sprouts	16 small new potatoes
4 Tbsp butter	3 Tbsp soy oil
3 Tbsp minced parsley	1/2 tsp grated lemon rind
4 Tbsp lemon juice	1 Tbsp minced chives
1/8 tsp black pepper	1/2 tsp salt
dash nutmeg	

Cook new potatoes in skins in 1/2 cup water until tender, but not mushy. In small pan heat butter. Add oil, parsley, chives and seasonings. Heat and stir in lemon rind and juice. Combine hot potatoes with lentil sprouts and pour sauce over them and serve hot. Makes 4 servings.

Red Cabbage with Adzuki Sprouts

2 cups adzuki bean sprouts	1 red tart apple, unpeeled and diced
4 strips bacon	
1/2 cup sliced onion	3 Tbsp wine vinegar
1 Tbsp sugar	1/2 tsp salt

1/8 tsp pepper   1 Tbsp caraway seeds
3 cups shredded red cabbage

Use large heavy skillet and fry bacon until crisp and remove from skillet. Add the cabbage and adzuki bean sprouts and stir to coat with bacon fat. Add cooking oil to make 3 Tbsp if there isn't enough bacon drippings. Stir-fry over medium heat for 3 minutes. Turn heat to low, cover and steam for 5 minutes. Add the apple, onion, mix well and steam for 3 minutes longer. Add the vinegar, sugar, salt and pepper and cooked bacon. Toss lightly to mix. Turn into serving dish and sprinkle with caraway seeds. Makes 6 servings.

Dilled Lentils and Zucchini

1 cup lentil sprouts   2 cups unpeeled zucchini
1/4 cup water   cut in 1/2 inch pieces
1/4 tsp salt   1 Tbsp dill weed
3 Tbsp butter   twist of two of black pepper

Cook zucchini in water 10 minutes or until tender, but firm. Add lentil sprouts and heat for 1 minute. Add remaining ingredients and toss lightly until butter is melted. Serve immediately. Makes 4 servings.

Soy Sprout Creole

2 cups soy sprouts   1/4 cup cold water
1/2 cup sliced green   1/2 cup sliced onion,
   celery   separate into rings
1 cup hot tomato juice   1/2 tsp salt
1/8 tsp pepper   1/8 tsp oregano
1 Tbsp soy sauce   1/8 tsp chili powder
1/2 tsp sugar   1 Tbsp cornstarch
1/4 cup water   1 Tbsp minced chives

Simmer soy sprouts in 1/4 cup water 30 minutes. Add hot tomato juice and celery and cook 5 minutes. Add onion rings and cook 5 minutes longer. Drain off tomato juice and thicken with cornstarch stirred into 1/4 cup cold water. Add seasonings, stir and cook 1 minute and carefully stir in cooked vegetables. Turn into serving dish, sprinkle with chives and serve immediately. Makes 4 servings.

Sauteed Lentil Sprouts

3 cups lentil sprouts	3 Tbsp butter
1/8 tsp salt	twist of black pepper
1/2 cup finely chopped onion	

Heat butter, but do not brown. Add lentil sprouts and onion and stir-fry over medium heat 5 minutes. Sprinkle with salt and pepper and cook 1 minute longer. Serve hot. Makes 4 servings.

Sprout Succotash

1-1/2 cups corn sprouts	paprika
1-1/2 cups lima bean sprouts	1/4 tsp salt
	1/4 cup water
twist or two of black pepper	4 Tbsp butter
1/2 cup milk	1/2 cup cream or canned milk
1 Tbsp cornstarch	1/4 cup cold water

Cook corn and bean sprouts in 1/4 cup water for 20 minutes or until tender. Add milk, cream, butter, salt and pepper. Stir cornstarch into cold water and add to sprout mixture, stirring over medium heat until thick and smooth. Sprinkle with paprika to serve. Makes 4 servings.

CHAPTER XVIII

RECIPES FOR DESSERTS

Chewy Soy Oatmeal Cookies

1-1/2 cup ground dried soy sprouts	2 Tbsp grated orange rind
1 cup shortening or butter	2 cups brown sugar
1 tsp vanilla	2 large eggs, beaten
1/2 tsp salt	1 cup flour
4 cups quick oatmeal	1 tsp soda
1 cup pitted dates	1 cup raisins
	1 cup coconut

Sift together flour, salt and soda. Cream together shortening and sugar until very light. Add the beaten eggs and vanilla and beat well. Stir in sifted dry ingredients and blend together. Stir in oatmeal, coconut and ground soy sprouts. Grind the raisins and dates and add to the batter. (Be sure to grind raisins and dates, as merely chopping them will make an entirely different cookie.) Drop from a teaspoon onto greased cookie sheets. Bake in a 350° oven for 10 to 12 minutes. Cookies will fall a little when taken out of the oven, but this makes them chewy. Makes about 5 dozen cookies.

Soy Crunchies

1 cup ground dried soy sprouts	2 tsp grated lemon rind
1 cup shortening	2 cups brown sugar
1/2 tsp salt	1 tsp soda
1 tsp lemon extract	1/2 tsp vanilla
2 cups oatmeal	2 eggs
3 cups flour	2 cups rice krispies
	1/2 tsp baking powder

Sift together dry ingredients. Cream sugar and shortening until light and fluffy. Add eggs and beat well. Stir in vanilla, lemon extract and lemon rind. Add flour mixture and blend well. Stir in soy nuts and then oatmeal and rice krispies. Drop by teaspoon onto greased cookie sheets. Bake in 375⁰ oven 12 to 15 minutes. Makes about 5 dozen cookies.

Currant Icebox Beanies

3/4 cup riced, cooked pinto bean sprouts	1/2 tsp salt
1 cup brown sugar	1/2 cup chopped pecans
1 beaten egg	1/2 cup shortening
1 tsp soda in 1 Tbsp boiling water	2 cups flour
1/2 tsp cloves	1/2 tsp cinnamon
	1/2 tsp nutmeg
	1 cup currants

Sift dry ingredients together, except soda. Cream sugar and shortening until light and fluffy and stir in egg. Add half of the sifted dry ingredients and mix well. Stir soda into boiling water and add to batter. Add remaining dry ingredients and stir in the currants and nuts. Turn out onto lightly floured waxed paper and form into a roll about 2 inches in diameter. Wrap in the waxed paper and chill in refrigerator at least 4 hours. Slice into 1/4 inch slices and bake in 350⁰ oven for 10 minutes or until lightly browned. Makes 4 dozen cookies.

Peanut Butter Bean Balls

1 cup mashed, cooked pinto bean sprouts	1/4 cup granulated sugar
1/2 cup shortening	1 cup peanut butter
2 cups brown sugar	2 beaten eggs
2 cups flour	1 tsp soda
1/2 tsp salt	1 tsp vanilla
2 Tbsp milk	1 cup dried, ground soy sprouts

Sift dry ingredients together. Cream shortening, peanut butter, brown sugar and vanilla until fluffy. Add beaten eggs and beat well. Blend in pinto bean sprouts. Add dry ingredients in thirds, beating after each addition. Add milk before last addition. Stir in ground dried soy sprouts. Chill one or two hours in refrigerator, and roll into balls the size of a walnut. Dip top in sugar and place on greased baking sheet. Flatten with fork dipped in flour. Bake in 375⁰ oven 8 to 10 minutes. Makes 5 dozen cookies.

Orange Bean Sprout Drops

1 cup cooked, mashed pinto bean sprouts	1 cup ground, dried soy sprouts
3/4 cup sugar	3/4 cup shortening
1 egg, beaten	2 tsp baking powder
2 cups unbleached flour	1 tsp vanilla
1/2 tsp salt	2 Tbsp grated orange rind

Sift dry ingredients together. Cream shortening, sugar and vanilla until light and fluffy. Add beaten eggs and bean sprouts and beat until smooth. Stir in dry ingredients one-third at a time. Stir in dried soy sprouts. Drop by teaspoon onto greased baking sheet. Bake in 350° oven for 12 to 15 minutes. Cool on racks. Frost with orange frosting.

Orange Frosting:

6 Tbsp soft butter or margarine	2 Tbsp grated orange rind
4 Tbsp orange juice (approx.)	1-1/2 cups sifted powdered sugar

Combine all ingredients and beat until smooth. Spread on cooled cookies.

Molasses Sprout Cookies

1-1/2 cups flour	3/4 tsp soda
1/2 tsp salt	1/2 cup margarine or shortening
3/4 cup brown sugar	1 egg, beaten
1/2 cup molasses	1/2 cup coconut
1/2 cup ground, roasted soy sprouts	

Sift flour, salt and soda together. Cream shortening and sugar until light. Add egg and beat well; stir in molasses and beat again. Stir in dry ingredients 1/3 at a time and mix thoroughly. Add the coconut and soy sprouts and blend. Drop by teaspoon onto greased baking sheet. Bake in 375° oven 10 to 12 minutes. Remove from pan while slightly warm. Makes 3 dozen cookies.

Soy Almond Cookies

2 cups flour
3/4 cup sugar
3/4 cup shortening
1 tsp baking powder
1 egg, beaten
2 Tbsp cream or canned
milk

2 tsp water
1/8 tsp salt
1/2 tsp almond extract
1/2 tsp vanilla extract
1 cup ground, dried
soy sprouts

Sift flour, baking powder and salt together. Stir in 1/2 cup ground soy sprouts. Cream sugar, shortening and vanilla and almond extract and add the egg. Stir in the flour-sprout mixture and knead with hands until smooth. Divide dough into 24 pieces and roll each one into a ball. Place on lightly greased cookie sheet and flatten with glass dipped in flour. Brush with cream and sprinkle with remaining 1/2 cup soy sprouts. Bake in 375° oven for about 12 minutes. Makes 2 dozen cookies.

Dutch Apple Sprout Pie

3-1/2 cups sliced
peeled apples
5 Tbsp flour
1/4 tsp nutmeg
2 Tbsp melted butter
3/4 cup brown sugar

1/4 tsp salt
1 cup evaporated milk
1/4 cup water
1 unbaked 9-inch pie
shell

Topping:

2 Tbsp brown sugar
1/8 tsp nutmeg

1/2 cup ground, dried
soy sprouts

Arrange apple slices in unbaked pastry shell. Mix together sugar, flour, salt, nutmeg, milk, water and melted butter. Pour over apples. Mix the topping together and sprinkle over top of pie. Bake in preheated 425° oven for 10 minutes. Reduce heat to 350° and continue baking 50 minutes. Cover with foil the last 30 minutes of baking. Cool before serving. Makes 1 pie or 6 to 8 servings.

Pinto Sprout Harvest Pie

1 cup mashed cooked pinto bean sprouts	1 large can evaporated milk
1/4 cup boiling water	3/4 cup brown sugar
1/2 tsp nutmeg	2 beaten eggs
1/2 tsp ginger	1/2 tsp salt
1/2 tsp cinnamon	1/4 tsp allspice
	1 unbaked 9-inch pie shell

Combine bean sprouts, sugar, salt, spices and eggs. Mix evaporated milk and boiling water together and gradually add to bean mixture. Pour into unbaked pie shell and bake in 350° oven for 45 minutes. Serve warm or cold with whipped cream if desired. Makes 1 pie or 6 to 8 servings.

Soy Sprout Pie

3/4 cup soy sprouts	3/4 cup fresh milk
1/2 cup brown sugar	1 cup evaporated milk
1/4 tsp salt	2 beaten eggs
1 tsp vanilla	1/2 cup shredded coconut
1/8 tsp nutmeg	1 unbaked 9-inch pie shell

Combine sprouts and fresh milk and blend in blender until sprouts are chopped fine, but not liquified. Mix with remaining ingredients, except nutmeg. Pour into unbaked pie shell, sprinkle with nutmeg and bake in 350° oven for 40 minutes or until knife comes out clean. Cool and top with whipped cream if desired. Makes 1 pie or 6 to 8 servings.

Apple Crunch

4 cups sliced apples	1/2 cup raisins or dates
2 Tbsp brown sugar	2 Tbsp lemon juice
1/4 tsp nutmeg	

Topping:

1/2 cup brown sugar	1/4 tsp salt
1 cup oatmeal	1/2 cup unbleached flour
1/2 cup dried soy sprouts, ground	6 Tbsp softened butter or margarine

Place sliced apples in 8 x 8" pyrex casserole. Sprinkle raisins, brown sugar, nutmeg and lemon juice over top. Combine remaining ingredients and mix until crumbly and spread evenly over top of apples. Bake in 350° oven 40 minutes. Makes 6 to 8 servings.

Cranberry Soy Sprout Crunch

1/2 cup dried ground soy sprouts	1 cup oatmeal
	1/2 cup flour
1/2 cup brown sugar	1/2 cup butter or
1/2 cup coconut	margarine
1 lb can whole cranberry sauce	1 Tbsp lemon juice

Mix together soy nuts, oatmeal, sugar, flour and coconut. Cut in butter until crumbly. Place half of mixture in buttered 8 x 8" baking dish. Combine cranberries and lemon juice and spread over mixture. Top with remaining crumb mixture. Bake in 350° oven for 45 minutes, Serve warm with whipped cream. Makes 6 or 8 servings.

Golden Honey Custard

1/2 cup soy sprouts	4 beaten eggs
1/3 cup honey	1 tsp vanilla
1/4 tsp nutmeg	2-1/2 cups milk

Blend soy sprouts and 1 cup milk until smooth. Combine with remaining milk, honey, eggs and vanilla. Pour into 1-1/2 quart baking casserole, sprinkle with nutmeg and place in pan of hot water. Bake in 375° oven for 50 to 60 minutes or when knife inserted in center comes out clean. Serve warm or cold. Makes 8 servings.

Fresh Apple-Soy Cake

1/2 cup ground soy sprouts	1 cup flour
1 tsp soda	1/2 tsp salt
1/2 tsp cinnamon	1/2 tsp nutmeg
1/2 tsp vanilla	1/4 cup shortening
3/4 cup brown sugar	1 beaten egg
2 cups chopped or coarsely grated apples	

Sift together flour, soda, salt, and spices. Cream shortening and sugar and blend in beaten egg. Stir in apples and ground sprouts. Add dry ingredients in thirds and blend well. Pour into 9 x 9" buttered baking pan and bake in 350° oven for 45 minutes. Serve warm with whipped cream or vanilla sauce. Makes 8 servings.

Vanilla Sauce

2 cups water	1 cup sugar, brown
4 tsp cornstarch	1/8 tsp salt
1 tsp vanilla	2 Tbsp butter

Combine sugar and cornstarch in sauce pan. Gradually add water and stir until blended. Cook over medium heat stirring constantly until thick and smooth. Remove from heat and add vanilla, salt and butter.

Pinto Pineapple Cake

1-1/2 cups cooked mashed pinto bean sprouts	1 cup well-drained crushed pineapple
1/4 cup butter	1 cup brown sugar
1 beaten egg	1-1/4 cup flour
1 tsp soda	1/2 tsp salt
2 tsp vanilla	1 cup chopped dates
1/2 cup chopped pecans	

Sift dry ingredients together. Cream sugar, butter and vanilla together until light. Add beaten egg and mix well. Stir in mashed bean sprouts, crushed pineapple and 1/3 of dry ingredients. Blend well and add remaining dry ingredients. Stir in dates and nuts. Pour into well-buttered 8 x 13 cake pan. Bake in 375° oven 35 to 40 minutes. Cool in pan. Frost with caramel frosting. Makes 12 servings.

Caramel Frosting

1 cup brown sugar	1/4 cup milk
1 cube butter	2 cups sifted powdered sugar
1 tsp vanilla	

Melt butter, add sugar and boil 2 minutes. Add milk and bring to boil again. Remove from heat and cool. Stir in vanilla and powdered sugar. Thin with hot water if too thick. Spread on cooled cake or cookies.

CHAPTER XIX

RECIPES FOR SNACKS AND CANDY

Soy Nut Fruit Balls

1 lb figs	1 lb raisins
1 lb dtaes	1-1/2 cup dried soy
1 can (No. 2-1/2) drained	sprouts, ground
crushed pineapple	1 cup coconut

Grind raisins, figs and dates with medium knife in food chopper. Add pineapple and soy sprouts and mix well. Form into small balls and roll in coconut. Store in tight container in cool place or in refrigerator. Makes 60 fruit balls.

Soy Peanut Butter Chews

1/2 cup peanut butter	1/2 cup honey
1/2 cup wheat germ	1/2 cup powdered milk
3/4 cup dried soy sprouts,	(not instant)
ground	1 cup coconut

Mix together powdered milk and wheat germ. Add peanut butter, honey and soy nuts. Roll into balls and roll in coconut. Store in covered container in refrigerator. Makes 36 chews.

Soy Nut Brittle

1-1/2 cup dried sprouts	1/4 cup water
coarsely chopped	1 cup sugar
1 cup corn syrup dark	1 tsp baking soda
2 Tbsp butter	

In a 2-quart saucepan stir together the sugar, corn syrup water and butter. Bring to a boil over medium heat, stirring constantly until sugar is dissolved. Reduce heat and cook without stirring until mixture reaches 300° on candy thermometer or until mixture forms a brittle ball when dropped in very cold water. Remove from heat, stir in chopped dried sprouts and then baking soda. Pour onto a buttered cookie sheet. Cool and break into pieces. Makes about 1-1/2 pounds.

Cracker Jack Popcorn

1-1/2 cups brown sugar	6 quarts popped corn
1/3 cup honey	2 cups roasted soy sprouts
1/4 cup molasses	3 Tbsp butter

In 2-quart saucepan stir together sugar, honey and molasses. Bring to boil over medium heat, stirring constantly until sugar is dissloved. Reduce heat and cook without stirring until mixture reaches 300° on candy thermometer or until mixture forms a brittle ball when dropped in very cold water. Remove from heat and stir in soy sprouts and butter. Pour over hot popped corn and stir to mix and coat corn. Turn out on buttered cookie sheets to cool. Break into pieces and store in covered container in cool place. Makes about 7 quarts of "cracker jack."

Garlic-Buttered Popcorn and Soy Nuts

4 cups popped corn	2 cups soy sprouts, dried
6 Tbsp butter	1 clove garlic, quartered
1/4 tsp salt	

Put butter and garlic into a skillet and heat until butter is melted, but not brown. Turn heat to very low and stir 3 minutes. Remove garlic and pour over popped corn and soy nuts. Sprinkle with salt. Makes 6 cups.

Soy Butterscotch Clusters

2 packages butterscotch chips	1 small can Chinese noodles (3 oz.)
1 cup roasted soy sprouts	

Melt butterscotch chips in couble boiler. Stir in soy sprouts and noodles. Keep over warm water to prevent hardening, and drop by teaspoon onto waxed paper. When hardened store in covered container in cool place. Makes about 25 clusters.

Soy Carob Fudge

1 cup roasted ground soy sprouts	2 egg yolks
	4 Tbsp carob powder

4 Tbsp butter	4 Tbsp honey
1-1/2 cup powdered milk (not instant)	2 or 3 Tbsp cream
	1 tsp vanilla

Cream butter and egg yolks with vanilla. Add small amounts of milk and carob powder alternately with honey and cream. Mix until creamy and thick. Add soy sprouts and stir in by hand. Pack into buttered shallow pan and chill in refrigerator. Cut into squares. Keep in covered container in refrigerator.

Variation: May be formed into rolls and sliced or formed into small balls and rolled in coconut. Maked 3/4 lb candy.

Sprout Fondant

1/2 cup hot unsalted mashed potatoes	1/2 cup butter
1 lb powdered sugar	1-1/2 cup powdered milk (not instant)
1 tsp vanilla	1 cup dried roasted ground soy sprouts

Add butter to hot potatoes and let cool. Add remaining ingredients, using 1 cup powdered milk and add enough of the remaining 1/2 cup as necessary. Mix well and knead with hands until smooth and creamy. Mix in the soy sprouts until evenly distributed. Mold into rolls, balls or any desired shape and chill in the refrigerator for one hour.

Variation: Coconut, fruit or cherries may also be added. Fondant can be dipped into chocolate, carob or caramel coating. Makes 1 pound.

BIBLIOGRAPHY

U. S. Department of Agriculture Handbook No. 8, *Composition of Foods*

U. S. Department of Agriculture Handbook No. 166, *How to Buy Meat for Your Freezer*

Courter, Gay, *The Beansprout Book:* Simon & Schuster, New York

Whyte, Karen Cross, *The Complete Sprouting Cookbook:* Troubador Press, San Francisco, California

Munroe, Esther, *Sprouts to Grow and Eat:* Stephen Greene Press, Brattleboro, Vermont

Hunter, Beatrice Trum, *The Natural Foods Cookbook:* Pyramid Communications, Inc., New York

Tobe, John H., *Sprouts: Elixir of Life:* Provoker Press, St. Catharine, Ontario

Dorothea Van Gundy Jones, *The Soybean Cookbook:* Arco Publishing Co., Inc., New York

Reynolds, Bruford Scott, *How to Survive with Sprouting:* Hawkes Publishing, Inc., Salt Lake City, Utah

Sprouts Recipe Book: Kitchen Garden, Salt Lake City, Utah

Nelson, Louise E., *Project Readiness:* Horizon Publishers, Bountiful, Utah

Dickey, Esther, *Passport to Survival:* Bookcraft Publishers, Salt Lake City, Utah

Elwood, Catharyn, *Feel Like a Million:* Pocket Books, New York

The Mother Earth News, Nov. 1971, *Sprouts: Miracle Food*

Sunset Magazine, Feb. 1974, *Sprouts Grow in the Kitchen*